Spencer West

with Susan McClelland

STANDING TALL

my journey

me to we
Better choices for a better world

Me to We
225 Carlton Street
Toronto ON Canada M5A 2L2
www.metowe.com/books

Distributed by
Greystone Books, D&M Publishers Inc.

Cataloguing in Publication data available
from Library and Archives Canada
ISBN: 978-1-55365-951-8 (pbk.)
ISBN: 978-1-55365-952-5 (ebook)

******

Cover and text design by Matthew Ng
Art Direction by Matthew Ng and Ryan Bolton
Cover photographs by Michael Rajzman
Printed and bound in Canada by Friesens
Text printed on 100% post-consumer, acid-free paper
Distributed in the U.S. by Publishers Group West

MIX
Paper from
responsible sources
FSC® C016245
FSC
www.fsc.org

STANDING TALL

my journey

I dedicate this book to anyone who has ever felt lost. Keep traveling, you will find your way again.

Foreword

Dear friends,

Along the journey of life, there are those unforgettable individuals who just "stick with you." People who, simply by having met them, enrich your life and leave you a stronger, better, more hopeful human being.

Spencer West is this person for us.

It is so easy to give up when faced with all the reasons why we can't do things. Across borders, from high-rise apartments to mud huts, people believe that they are not rich enough, or smart enough, or powerful enough to make a change. The media sells us on this idea, leading us to accept that only the perfect or the beautiful or the famous can leave an impression on the world.

Spencer West redefines what is possible every single day— not only what it means to stand tall as a human being, but what it means to excel as a citizen of this world.

From the first moment he met us and gave each of us a giant hug—yes, a giant hug—to seeing him do a cartwheel and share stories of being a high school cheerleader, to watching him inspire tens of thousands of students as a motivational speaker, he's the real deal.

This book shares the story of Spencer's life journey, a journey that has taken him halfway around the world and back again. From Wyoming to Kenya to Toronto to India, from a happy and optimistic child, to a struggling teen, to a hometown hero, to a role model for thousands. Spencer has really lived; he's taken it all in and when a barrier—physical or otherwise—arises, he's the first to tackle it with a smile.

We hope that parents will share this story with their children, and friends with their friends, passing on this moving example of what makes a life worth living. It's one of those seldom stories that truly transcends age.

For us, Spencer is nothing less than a hero, a bright soul, and someone who inspires others wherever he goes. We still recall the first time we saw him speak to an auditorium stuffed with students. After he was introduced, this little guy in a wheelchair just zipped onto the stage. With a huge grin, he emanated confidence. And the first thing that comes out of his mouth—in true Spencer West fashion—is a joke about losing his legs in a freak magician accident having his legs sawed off. After that speech, the line up to meet Spencer rounded the corner.

The best part is that Spencer is the same guy on or off the stage. None of it is an act—he's just a guy with an unbelievable personality who won't back down when faced with a wall.

If all of us had his courage, inspiration and willingness to overcome obstacles, think what a different place the world could be. We'd see that our uniqueness is our gift, and that no limits—physical or otherwise—can hold us back in achieving our dreams.

Craig and Marc Kielburger
Co-founders
Free The Children & Me to We

Introduction

As soon as I got off the plane, it hit me. The air. It smelled of roadside fires, diesel fuel and perspiration. The Kenyan sun was different than the one in Arizona, too. It was higher in the sky and beat down along with a humid wind that washed over me as I headed into the terminal. But once inside, I nearly choked on the lack of air. I breathed in and out deeply and looked around. Adults of all shapes and sizes were talking in languages I did not recognize. Children were running up and down the corridor, some playing tag, others kicking a soccer ball. All of them were laughing with great smiles spread across their faces. There were so many people, and making so much commotion, it was almost like being in New York's Grand Central Station.

I was one of the first people in line to meet the customs officer, a burly man in a baby blue cotton shirt and dark blue slacks. I handed him my passport and took in his nametag, which I could not read. He noticed my stare.

"You speak English? Why are you here?" he asked, with a thick accent.

I looked up into his dark brown eyes. "I... I... I," I stuttered.

The man smiled. His big, toothy grin put me at ease.

"Can you tell me why you have come to Nairobi?" he said.

"I am here to build a school," I finally replied, unsure as to why I felt so uneasy.

"Where?"

"The Maasai Mara."

The man, still smiling, looked me up and down, with a puzzled expression on his face. "When do you leave for the Maasai Mara?"

"Well, I'm staying here in Nairobi for two days and then we're flying to the Mara on Monday morning."

"Ahhh, I see," he said, stamping my passport. But his grip remained on my passport, as he handed it back to me. *Tell me... why are you really here?*" I imagined him saying, as he stared with intensity into my own dark brown eyes.

I started to shake. He wasn't letting go. *I'm... I'm a good person*, I thought to myself. *I'm just here to build a school. Why won't he give me my passport?*

I then heard a voice in my head—maybe his voice—saying to me: *"But you're here for something else, too. You will find the answer. Africa has a way of calling people back to themselves."*

Letting go of my passport at last, the customs officer smiled and let me enter Nairobi.

I was in Kenya.

That was in March 2008. For several years leading up to my trip to Kenya, I had been feeling restless. My life has never been ordinary. My list of youthful accomplishments include being one of the only males on an all-female cheerleading squad and winning a state championship, performing in musicals, being featured on state-wide television, winning awards for my volunteer work and grades. But I think what you may perceive as most un-ordinary about me is that I have done all these things without the use of my legs. I was born with sacral agenesis, a rare disorder, which, in my case, resulted with little control or use of my legs. At the age of three, doctors began amputating my legs until they were little longer than the size of two large eggplants. (A vegetable I'm not the biggest fan of, to be honest).

Despite that, somehow, through the greatness of my family, my friends and the supportive people in the small-town Wyoming community where I was born and raised, I thrived. I would never have accomplished any of the above had it not been for them. I was never treated differently. I was just Spencer J. West. A whopping 2'7" tall, who drove a car too fast. Who went to all of his proms with his best friend, Marci. I'm just a little guy with big dreams and buckets of courage. And I like to laugh a lot.

But in the years leading up to Kenya, I had found myself living a somewhat conventional life: working a stable job, earning a good income, yet employed in an industry that didn't challenge me, or even appeal to me very much. I felt like I was drowning. Yet I knew every person on this planet was here for a reason. I knew that I too had a purpose. A calling.

One small problem: I didn't know what that was.

My good friend Reed Cowan had been telling me almost since the day I first met him in 2002 that I should be a motivational speaker. That I could inspire people. At the time, I was an undergraduate communications studies student at Westminster College in Salt Lake City, Utah. I was also working part time as a clerk at an Old Navy store. Reed swaggered in on that wintry day and we quickly became close friends.

"Public speaker!" he would say over and over again. "That's your calling! You inspire people!"

"I am so boring. Who would want to hear me speak?" I would typically respond.

No one else had any other suggestions of what it is that I was called to do in this world, and at the time I certainly couldn't figure it out for myself. So, like many young people, I settled into a funk. I just existed. My life had no passion. Then Reed asked if I would come to Kenya to help him and his family build a school for Free The Children. At first, I didn't know if it was such a good idea.

At the end of that first trip to Kenya, after a dinner of stew and rice, I sat out on the stone patio of the center where Free The Children works. I had had such an amazing trip. So many things happened that touched the core of my heart and got me thinking of my life's purpose. I thought about one little girl I met in the village of Emori Joi, who said she didn't know white people could suffer too—like me, living my life without legs. I thought about my loving family, who never made me feel like I was handicapped.

"Why are you really here?" I whispered to myself.

And then it hit me. It hit me just like that warm Kenyan air for the first time when we landed.

Reed was right. I could inspire people to do whatever they wanted. To love who they were despite what they looked like, where they were born or who they were born to. In the end, aren't we all unique and special? I just happened to wear my differences on the outside, because I had no legs.

I then remembered a passage I read in *The Alchemist*, a book by Paulo Coelho:

"... before a dream is realized, the Soul of the World
tests everything that was learned along the way. It does
this not because it is evil, but so that we can, in addition to realizing our dreams, master the lessons we've
learned as we've moved toward that dream. That's the
point at which most people give up."

But I had refused to give up. Just like the shepherd in *The Alchemist*, I discovered that my path has always been right in front of me—since the very first day I was born.

Chapter 1

No one heard me arrive in the world. At least, no one from *my* family. As my parents explained to me, I was a planned C-section because an ultrasound showed I was breeched, meaning I was sitting upright, not positioned with my head down, ready to be born. (I have always liked to do things my way.) My Mom had passed out from the medication the doctors gave her. My Dad, Kenny, was sitting outside the operating room of Memorial Hospital of Sweetwater County in a stiff metal chair, reading the sports section of the *Rock Springs Daily Rocket-Miner*, the town newspaper. Unlike today, family members, including Dads, were not allowed to be in the operating room when a woman was delivering her baby via surgery.

I was born on January 7, 1981, at 7:50 a.m. to be exact. I am a Capricorn, born in the Chinese year of the monkey, which means I am clever, flexible and agile. These are all true traits, of course, including the walking on my hands as a monkey part.

Doctors told my mother that they would do the C-section as soon as she felt labor pains. She thought she had, starting at about midnight, when a few waves of pain washed over her abdomen and then went away. She woke my father, who was sleeping beside her in the home they had recently bought close to the elementary school. It was time.

Dad had spent the first few months of my Mom's pregnancy asking for advice from his friends and relatives with children and the women at Desert Oil, the company where Dad worked. He asked what Mom's delivery would be like and what were good "boy" names, since he was hoping I would be a boy. He went with Mom to the furniture store to pick out a brown wooden crib and helped stock the closet in the nursery with diapers, brand new pajamas and baby sweaters and blankets.

But for the last few weeks of the pregnancy, Dad's enthusiasm for my birth carried with it a tone of concern. He would place his right ear on my mother's ballooning stomach, then he would rise and say, "Something is not right."

"Oh, for Pete's sake," my Mom would reply, waving my Dad away. "You're being ridiculous."

"No, Tonette," Dad would press. "Why don't we feel anything? Why is he not kicking?"

"I've felt him kicking."

"When? Tell me *when* you've felt him kicking."

My Mom would look up at the ceiling fan. "Well, when I

feel the kicking it is kind of like a butterfly—I feel one kick immediately followed by another," she said. "I'm not sure whether I am feeling feet, knees or elbows. But I am feeling ... something."

"The ladies at Desert Oil say you're supposed to be feeling big, huge kicks that knock you over," my Dad pressed.

"Kenny," Mom sighed. "Dr. Pryich says the baby is fine. All the ultrasounds have come back showing that the baby is healthy, other than that he or she is still in the wrong position."

"Come on, Tonette," Dad continued. "Look real close at those photos from the ultrasound machine. You can't tell anything about our son from those."

To Dad's credit, years later, when I looked at those photographs, I'm surprised they could have seen I was even in the breech position. The machines were not what they are today—a child's development is now monitored bone by bone. All I looked like in my mother's womb is a bunch of squiggly white lines with a big alien-like head.

"You had a big head then and you have a big head now," my sister, Annie, would joke many years later, when my mother dug out her big photo albums wrapped with bright red and yellow ribbons.

"We have a baby," my Dad, Aunt Jamie and my Mom's parents, Grandma and Grandpa Callas, heard a nurse say from the other side of the swinging operating room doors. Everyone immediately perked up and waited for the doors to open.

After what seemed like an eternity, Dr. Climaco came out

into the waiting room, holding me wrapped in a baby blue blanket and wearing a matching wool bonnet.

"Kenny," Dr. Climaco said as he handed me to my Dad. "It's a boy."

"Wonderful!" chanted Dad and Grandpa in unison.

"Yes, but we have a problem," Dr. Climaco continued, with a change of tone in his voice.

"Oh," said my grandmother stepping up to look at me. "What is it?"

"The child is absolutely perfect from the waist up," he said. "But from the waist down, he seems to have a deformity of some sort."

"What kind of deformity?" my father asked, not taking his eyes off of me.

"I'm not sure if he is going to walk."

On the day I was born, my aunt Jamie, an honor student, decided to do something she never did: she skipped morning classes. She decided to show up late for Ms. Vincent's Grade 10 English course hoping to be one of the first people to hold me. Jamie never missed school. She did homework on holidays, and, during summer breaks, read her literature books in advance, like Emily Bronte's *Wuthering Heights* and Ayn Rand's *The Fountainhead*.

After Dad held me and then my grandma and grandpa took their turns, Jamie clutched me close to her chest so Dr. Climaco could talk to the others about my legs.

"I... I... I don't understand. Can you explain, Doc, what you think is wrong with him?" Jamie overheard my father say.

"You will need to go to Salt Lake City. It is the closest city to Rock Springs that provides the type of medical testing and treatment facilities you are looking for," Dr. Climaco replied. "I don't have the answers myself. Whatever is wrong with your son's legs is not my area of expertise."

Jamie, still holding me, walked over to Dad and Grandma Callas, who were standing side by side.

"It's OK, Kenny," said my grandmother. "We will all be there to support you and Tonette. Whatever you need, we will help you get it."

After Dr. Climaco left, my father sat down with a sigh and covered his face with his hands. He then took a deep breath and looked up. *"I know,"* he said more optimistically. "We will get through this."

Jamie returned to school and proudly announced to the entire class, as well as Ms. Vincent, who were all eager to learn the news, that I was a boy and had been named Spencer. Jamie then took her seat beside Phillip, her boyfriend of two years.

"Phillip," Jamie whispered as Ms. Vincent asked the class questions about their reading, Shakespeare's *Romeo and Juliet*. "Phillip, Spencer is so beautiful. He has long, black hair, just like all of us did. But—" she trailed off.

"What is it?" Phillip asked.

"There is something wrong with his legs."

"Ms. West, Ms. West. Tonette, Tonette," said a dark-haired

nurse with rosy cheeks. She was gently shaking my mother's shoulder. "Tonette, it's time to wake up."

A few hours had passed since my Dad first held me and heard the news from Dr. Climaco that something wasn't right with my legs. Now the nurse was trying to get my mother to wake up to tell her the news. After the surgery, the nurses had moved her from the operating room to a private room. She slowly opened her eyes, shading them at first from the sunlight streaming in the window.

"You have a son, Ms. West," the nurse said. My father stood by the head of the bed, while the nurse fluffed my mother's pillows and helped her sit up.

Another nurse eventually placed me on the bed beside her. She immediately rolled over and held me.

"Tonette," Dad eventually said, slowly. "The doctor says there is something wrong with Spencer."

"Oh," said Mom, scratching her eyes. "So you've decided on the name Spencer I see."

"Spencer James, of course," he added. "James after your Dad."

Dr. Pryich, who was Mom's main physician and present for my delivery, walked into the room. "Tonette," he said, pulling up a chair beside my mother and placing a hand on her arm. "There is a problem with your son."

"What problem?" whispered Tonette as she began to peel the blanket off of me.

"Well, we're not exactly sure," Dr. Pryich said, looking at my Dad. "We think…"

The door to the room swung open and in walked Grandpa

West, my Dad's Dad, chewing on a cigar imported from Cuba. "I hear we have a baby! Can I take a look at him?"

"Yes, Dad," my father replied. "Spencer is finally here."

"So the baby is a boy!" my grandfather declared. "And you're going with Spencer, from the movie *Spencer's Mountain*. I remember the catchphrase of that film: *The world steps aside to let a man pass, if he knows where he is going.* I guess this little guy will go far in life!"

"Actually, Keith, I got the name from a book of baby names," Mom interjected.

"No, Tonette. I picked it from the movie," replied my Dad.

At that point, Grandma West pushed open the door and walked in carrying a vase of white lilies. "Do we have a grandson?" she quipped.

"Yes, Mom," said my Dad.

"Let me see the baby," she said, hurrying over to my Mom's bed.

Dr. Climaco eventually had the opportunity to explain to my mother that my legs, while they appeared to have some movement, didn't have the muscle control that the legs of a healthy baby would have. My legs also hung in such a manner that, as my Dad put it, looked like I had frog's legs. Lucky for me, it didn't matter one bit to my parents or the rest of the family. They accepted me for who I was—their Spencer.

Mom and I had to stay in the hospital for a week so that her incision could heal properly. But the whole time she was thinking: *I want to go home with my baby. I want to start our life together as a family.*

To this day, Mom says she was never in denial: "It didn't matter to me what you looked like. You were mine." One of my earliest memories, in fact, is of my Mom looking down at me with her soft, doe-like brown eyes and running her cool fingers over my forehead.

At some point during that week, Dr. Pryich informed Mom and Dad that he had booked an appointment for me at the University of Utah College of Medicine in Salt Lake City. "They'll run some tests there," he said. "The doctors will give you the diagnosis and then come up with the best course of treatment. We don't know much at this stage, we just have our suspicions," he then added. "So please be prepared for anything."

A week after Mom and I left the hospital, my parents drove me the three hours from Rock Springs to Salt Lake City in Utah. It was an unseasonably warm and sunny winter day, they tell me. I was asleep in my car seat, bundled up in some blankets. Mom was tired too, from spending several hours every night up with me. She says the longest I ever slept at one time, for at least the first six months of my life, was three hours. (What can I say? I loved the night life.)

Dad, trying to keep Mom from dozing off, recounted hunting stories. She'd heard them all many times, so it didn't work. Nonetheless, he would keep trying with the same stories.

When they arrived at the hospital, Mom and Dad had to wait nearly six hours for one of the doctors to see me. Dad read the newspapers, while Mom rocked me back and forth in her arms.

Once I was admitted, Mom was dealt her first emotional blow since she gave birth. She wasn't allowed to spend the night with me. I had to remain in the hospital alone, while the doctors ran some tests.

Dad had to pry me out of Mom's arms and hand me to a nurse. Mom cried the entire ride down the elevator, all the way to Verna's house—she was my Grandpa West's sister-in-law, who lived in Salt Lake City. Mom slept fitfully the rest of that day and all that night, tossing and turning, knowing that no one could take care of me as well as she could.

Mom and Dad were back at the hospital the moment visitors were allowed the next day. Within a few hours, doctors told them that I had sacral agenesis, abnormal development of the spine. I had a serious form of the illness, too. X-rays showed that my entire sacrum—the bones at the bottom of the spine that form a triangle and connect, in layman's terms, my back-bones to my leg bones—was missing. "I don't think he will ever sit up," one doctor told my Mom and Dad.

Another doctor at the hospital said I would be lucky if I lived until I was a teenager, as children with such severe cases of sacral agenesis rarely do.

Yet a more optimistic doctor wrote in my file that my parents would have to "plan that the child will have to be basically sedentary, so they should help him develop interests in music, reading and writing."

As the doctors ran one final test on me, Mom and Dad waited outside in the lobby. Mom started to cry. "I just don't believe it," she sobbed. "He will live longer than a teenager. I just know it!"

Tears fell from my Dad's eyes, too. "He's young, Tonette. Doctors are always making great strides in science. He will live a long life!"

As my parents have told me many times, they were then given a reminder, right there in the hospital, of just how lucky they were to have me. Their attention was suddenly drawn to a woman wailing into the receiver of the black pay telephone on the wall.

"Honey, honey," the woman cried. "She has a brain tumour. She's not going to live the year! She's just a baby... I... I..."

The woman's legs gave way and she collapsed on the floor. Two nurses rushed to her side and helped guide her to a nearby room.

When the lobby was quiet again, Mom looked into my father's tired and bewildered eyes.

"We are so lucky," she whispered to him. "That woman isn't going to get her child for even a year. We will have Spencer for many."

All the way back to Rock Springs, Dad's mind churned over the doctor's diagnosis. He was a sportsman and he summed it up in this way: the pitcher in the game of life had thrown Dad a curve ball. The game he hoped to be playing as a Dad had suddenly changed. Sulking off to the bench was not an option. He would play by the new rules.

As for Mom, I was her son. She felt connected to me long before the doctor delivered me. She didn't need to force herself to see beyond my disability. She already did. She saw my potential as a human being from the get-go. And it was this immediate acceptance of me, the way I was, that would influence me the most as a child.

Chapter 2

Within a week of returning from my first trip to Salt Lake City I started to develop colic. Several times during the day, and most of the night, I wailed uncontrollably. Mom lost all the weight she gained from her pregnancy, just by carrying me up and down the stairs, as the motion of going up and down was the only thing that would calm me, stopping my screaming.

Starting when I was about six months old, Mom would bundle me up, strap me in the car seat and go to the arts and crafts shops to buy supplies. She would then spend the few hours during the day when I *did* sleep creating photo albums or sewing T-shirts and pajamas for me. Mom didn't go back to work—she stayed home with me until I started kindergarten. But she was worried about money, at least at first. Medical care in the United States is very costly. The type of treatment the doctors said I needed could have run into the six digits and put my Mom and Dad into debt for life. One of the doctors in

Salt Lake City who confirmed my diagnosis, Dr. Coleman, suggested that they take me to the Shriners Hospital for Children, also in Salt Lake City, where he held a position. In the United States—as well as Canada, Mexico and Panama—the Shriners fraternity has built many hospitals that offer free treatment for children, especially those with orthopedic needs.

There were only two prerequisites: my Mom and Dad needed to show that it would be difficult, if not impossible, for them to pay for treatment, which was true. The other prerequisite was that a member of the Shriners had to sponsor me, which wasn't difficult. Rock Springs was a small town and word soon reached Don Thomas and Bill McCurtain, both long-term members of the Shriners Club and friends of the family. They came forward and agreed to sponsor me.

A few weeks later, my Mom received a phone call from an administrator at the Shriners Hospital saying my application had been approved and I could come in for an appointment. Within four months of my birth, I was back on the road to Salt Lake City for another round of doctors' visits.

"Have you ever done this before?" Mom asked Dr. Coleman, who became my main physician at the Shriners Hospital. Dr. Coleman had re-examined me and he disagreed with the original and grim prognosis. He didn't just believe I wouldn't be able to sit up, but that I could walk with the use of prosthetic legs.

"Have you ever done this kind of treatment before?" Mom asked Dr. Coleman again, for he was now recommending that my legs be amputated just above the knees, so that the prosthetic legs could fit me best.

"No," he eventually replied, matter-of-factly, looking up from the pile of papers in front of him. "I have only ever known of five patients with a problem like Spencer's. So no, I have never done this course of treatment before."

Dr. Coleman then stood up and walked over to an X-ray machine. He switched on the light and gestured for my parents to come closer. "You can see how Spencer's legs are jutting out from his pelvis bone like so," he continued, using his hand to gesture the direction. "My plan is to amputate his legs just above the knee, right about here," he said, pointing to the spot. "I will then want him to wear a special contraption every night for about a year, which will help straighten out the bones in the legs, so that they are more horizontal. Right now, the way Spencer's legs are descending from the pelvis, they go out to the side and gently rise up, almost as if he was sitting in the yoga lotus pose. But once this is corrected, I don't see anything holding him back from walking."

"OK, doc," Dad said, taking his hat off. "When do we have the surgery?"

"Not until he is about three," Dr. Coleman said, switching off the X-ray and returning to his swivel chair.

"What do we do in the meantime?" Mom asked. "I mean, what do we do over the next three years? What can we expect?"

"We'd like to see Spencer every three months," Dr. Coleman replied. "And what you need to do at home is focus on getting him to talk, read and communicate. Expose him to music and the arts."

Barbara, who was the prosthetic coordinator for the hospital, was in the room with Mom, Dad and Dr. Coleman. She opened a photo album full of pictures of children and teens wearing prosthetic hands, arms and legs. Almost all of the photographs showed kids with smiling faces.

"It isn't the end of the world for Spencer to have to wear prosthetic legs," she said, looking first at my Mom and then my Dad. "Lots of famous people were missing a limb or limbs, like Canadian runner Terry Fox. Despite their physical disabilities, many people have gone on to accomplish great things in life. Disabilities can keep your son down, or he can rise above them. Mexican painter Frida Kahlo had permanent disabilities from a bus accident and may have had spina bifida. U.S. president Franklin Roosevelt was paralyzed from the waist down from a bout of childhood polio."

"What about the doctor who told us that Spencer might not live past his teenage years?" Mom asked. "He said that children with Spencer's form of sacral agenesis often have kidney failure."

"That's true," said Dr. Coleman. "And an unfortunate possibility. You will just have to be vigilant, and whenever you suspect there is an infection, go to your local doctor or the hospital as soon as possible."

Mom was torn. Her motherly, intuitive side just knew I was going to live a long, prosperous life. But in her mind, the words that I might not live past my teenage years haunted her. She tried to shake her doubts away, but over time they would creep back. Mostly, she did whatever she could to stay active and not think about my future.

Mom spent the first summer of my life walking me in a stroller around the neighborhood. She came to like the summers best, because I could wear shorts. Winter clothing was more challenging. Because my legs were at such an awkward angle, she couldn't get regular pants to fit me. During the winter, when we were housebound due to snowstorms, she would put me in a one-piece nightgown that tied with a string at the bottom. Mom picked up stretchy velour pants and sweatpants at the discount stores, and my great aunt Antonia began making pants for me by cutting open the bottom half of the side seams and inserting extra panels of material. It would look like I was wearing bell-bottoms, very fashionable at the time for babies. Yet my feet never really grew, so my socks and shoes were always those that would fit a newborn.

Often, when Mom would be out walking with me, people would peer into my stroller and gasp. "Is he OK?" they would ask. "What is wrong with him?"

At first Mom would reply politely and explained my diagnosis. But when the whispers, stares and enquiries kept coming, she grew impatient. "He was born that way," she would say, and then quickly move on, so the onlookers didn't have anything to gape at.

By one-year-old, I had mastered crawling. By two-years-old I could lift up my torso, and "walk" everywhere, using my hands as if they were my feet. I didn't feel I was missing anything. I would simply put one hand in front of the other and march forward. On many occasions, my Dad took me for a dip in the cool, dark lake at Grandpa West's cabin. I played outside with other kids, getting around for the first little while in a red miniature toy car that was battery powered. I'd make my way from the dining room to the kitchen to grab a snack and then back to prop myself up in front of *Scooby-Doo* faster than Kyle from down the street could pour himself a glass of milk. One upside to not having any legs was that I developed, by age three, the arm strength of an Olympic weightlifter. And, like a true child born of the year of the monkey, I could swing myself up onto the backs of couches and climb up people's backs, too—like Phillip's.

Jamie and her boyfriend Phillip frequently babysat me, and I loved it, because I used to pretend Phillip was a piece of equipment at the jungle gym in the park. I would heave myself up onto his back or shoulders and he would race around the house at top speed, just like Dad would do before bedtime. One time, while racing Jamie down the stairs with me tucked in his arms, Phillip fell and tumbled from the second to the first floor. After we landed, he immediately sat up, rolled me over, felt every bone in my tiny body and searched my face for any sign that I had endured trauma of any kind. (Not co-incidentally, he became a doctor.) He breathed a sigh of relief when he discovered I was OK. "I thought I had hurt you," he said, looking over at Jamie.

"No way, Uncle Phillip," I giggled. "I am not hurt. Don't you know? I *am Superman!*"

Not all of my earliest memories, however, are of such fun

times. For as long as I can remember, I have had difficulty sleeping. I can't make it through an entire night without waking up. Mom says it's the way I have always been. I, however, trace my sleep woes to when I was three. It was the first time I remember being in the hospital overnight without Mom or Dad by my side. It was for my first major surgery, when Dr. Coleman amputated the bottom part of my legs. I don't recall much about the surgery, except the blinding lights in the operating room.

But it is not this memory that keeps me awake at night. Rather, it is of being alone—the moment my Mom left the hospital when visiting hours ended, when her fingers slowly loosened their grip on mine and the lights in the children's ward were turned low. I started to whimper, and continued until I was so exhausted that I fell asleep. Like my Mom did when she was away from me, I tossed and turned all night long. I would wake up, find myself alone and cry out for my mother. She never came. I felt her absence like a brick of cement in the bottom of my stomach. While I had become accustomed to not being able to use my legs, not having my greatest support by my side, my mother, was too much.

Before I left the hospital, my mother says I met the engineer, Ron, who would design the contraption I'd wear after the wounds from my surgery healed. The contraption—and it was very much so a contraption—that was to straighten out my legs would be made out of a hard plastic and fit around my waist with an elastic-like band. It would also wrap around the bottom of the stumps of my legs. He took some gooey, plastic moulds of my torso and then explained that the device would look much like a bucket. Ron then apparently showed me a pair of artificial legs that would be similar to the ones I would eventually wear. "You'll see," my Mom says he told me. "You'll be walking real soon."

The next morning, my Mom says I woke earlier than usual. My hands stretched to feel the white bandages wrapped around whatever parts of my legs I still had left. I started to cry. "Mom!" I called out in a loud voice. She came into my room moments later, wiping her tired eyes, her hair frizzy and knotted from sleeping. She smiled and lifted me into her arms. She then carried me to our rec room where she turned on *Mr. Rogers' Neighborhood*. My tears slowly went away as Mr. Rogers sang his trademark song, "It's a Beautiful Day in the Neighborhood." All the while, Mom held me on her lap and rubbed my back, rocking me in a mahogany rocking chair.

"Spencer, what do you want to be when you grow up?" Mom asked me during a commercial.

"Superman!" I replied in a bold, confident voice, not taking my eyes off the television. "Or, maybe Batman!"

Mom laughed. "Well you already are a *super*man," she responded. "What kind of powers are you going to have?"

"I am going to leap off tall buildings. I am going to learn to fly."

Mom hugged me tightly. "Well, I will do whatever I can to help you," she said. "But promise me one thing. Until your incisions are healed and you're feeling better, don't try jumping off anything."

"OK," I replied as *Mr. Rogers* came back on.

After a while, Mom laid me down on a cushion on the couch and went into the kitchen. I could hear the coffee machine percolating. But what I couldn't hear was Mom talking on the telephone to her sister, Jamie, who was by that time studying business at the University of Wyoming. "I just feel I need to do something," my Mom said. "I think getting a second opinion would give me peace of mind."

Jamie replied that she and Phillip had also talked about Spencer and his course of treatment, and both agreed that my parents should get a second opinion.

"Thank you for being on my side," whispered Mom. Then, in a stronger voice, she declared: "Superman's mother, Lara, sent her son to Earth to escape the destruction of Krypton. She remained behind, however, trusting somehow that Superman would be OK. I, on the other hand, will be there every step of the way with my little superman!"

"What are you talking about?" Jamie asked, laughing.

"Oh, sorry, Spencer and I have been watching too much television lately."

For the first few weeks after the surgery, I couldn't do much at all, except lie down, watch television; lie down, watch the birds fly overhead in my stroller; lie down, watch the buildings zoom past through the car's windows. Unbeknownst to me, Mom had called several orthopedic specialists in the United States. During quiet moments in the afternoon, when sometimes I'd nap but more often than not I'd watch *Bugs Bunny* and other cartoons, Mom would make phone calls and type out letters to doctors. She waited nervously for responses. Finally, a doctor in California called. "I agree with Dr. Coleman," he said, and then added: "You're in the best hands possible at the Shriners."

Mom thanked him for his time and hung up the phone, not feeling very relieved.

Another doctor agreed to look at my file, but echoed the California specialist's comment. "Dr. Coleman's a good doctor. I don't think you want to switch."

After Mom hung up the phone, she turned and saw me standing. For the first time since the surgery, in the middle of the doorway leading into the kitchen, I was standing. I had lifted my torso up and walked on my hands, as if I hadn't just had a major operation. One of the bandages from my legs had unravelled and was trailing behind me. Once again I lifted my torso up by my arms, and I swung my legs around. Then I sat down, upright.

"Mom," I said in a loud, confident voice. "Can I have a snack?"

It was, in fact, easier for me to swing my amputated legs, now half the size from before, than my full legs. Still, Mom was a bit apprehensive the first time I went out into the garage, plopped myself on my red skateboard and went tearing down the driveway at top speed. She watched me closely from the porch, shaking her head and smiling to herself. (In his spare time, it is hardly known, but Superman was a skateboarder).

From then on, Mom was always dragging me in early from playing in the backyard—not out of concern, but because my white bandages were covered in dirt and grass stains. But after a bath and new bandages, I usually headed right back outside to play.

It took only a few days from when I first rolled off the couch, manoeuvred my way into the kitchen and asked for a snack for Mom to go through about six packages of bandages. Soon, I started discarding them completely, often leaving them strewn on the driveway or the front lawn for Dad, returning from work, to pick up.

One spring evening after dinner, when Mom was washing the dishes and Dad was in the garage changing the oil on the Cadillac, I opened the front screen door and skidded out onto the porch. I heard the telephone ring as I made my way across the grass to the sidewalk. I stopped an inch from the curb and picked up some pebbles that were lying on the street.

Mom was talking to her friend Jo on the telephone. Jo lived across the street and called asking to borrow some sugar for the blueberry muffins that she was baking.

"Tonette," she said to Mom. "I'm looking out the window and I see Spencer on the street."

Mom stretched the telephone cord as far as it would go and then reached over and pulled open the sheer living room curtains. She spied me down at the very edge of the curb tossing stones, trying to skip them, like Grandpa West did at the lake.

Mom banged on the windowpane. I looked up and waved. She smiled and then resumed her conversation with Jo.

Shortly after Mom hung up the telephone, Grandma Callas called. "I got a call from Jo across the street saying that Spencer is down by the road. Tonette, he's going to get hurt. Cars can't see him. Go and get him."

"Mom," she replied, shaking her head. "Spencer is a little boy and he is going to do little boy things. He doesn't think he's any different than any other child. I want him to throw rocks and to pretend he is Superman. I want him—" Mom paused. "I want him to be happy."

We returned to Salt Lake City a few months after my surgery. We were picking up the device that had been made for me, which Ron and Dr. Coleman wanted me to wear every night in an attempt to straighten out the remaining parts of my legs.

As we entered Intermountain Limb and Brace, which was the facility that would make my legs and where Ron had taken the moulds for my brace, I got a good look around at my surroundings. I didn't recall much about the lab from my first visit, except the cool, slippery sensation of Ron taking the plaster casts, which he would use to make the device. Now, I took everything in: the shelves filled with real-looking fake hands, fake arms, fake fingers, fake legs and fake skin. The trays filled with nails, screwdrivers and pieces of plastic and paint.

I swallowed hard.

"Mom, Mom," I whispered, as she held me in her arms. "Am I going to have to wear those?" I asked, pointing a shaking finger at a pair of legs. The sides of them were skin-colored, like the real-looking fake legs. The fronts, however, were gleaming silver screws and pulleys, held together by red, black and yellow wire. They looked like the legs of C-3PO from *Star Wars*.

"Spence, I'm not sure," she stammered.

"Hello, ladies and gentlemen!" Ron said, rushing out from one of the rooms. He was wearing a long white lab coat with his typically messy dark hair. He bent down and shook my hand. "I hear you are doing really, really well," he beamed, as I nodded. "This is great news! OK. Let's begin."

Ron held up the contraption he wanted me to wear. It did look like a bucket. Ron had me lie down on the cot in the room and he showed my Mom how to put it on me. The hard plastic dug into my skin, and the straps pulled on my legs and made me so uncomfortable that my instinct was to pick at the device and try to remove it. Ron stressed over and over how important it was for me to wear it every night, and even during the day—if I was at home and not doing anything.

Mom listened attentively. "Ah-ha. Ah-ha. Ah-ha," she kept saying, while Dad looked over her shoulder. I just lay there on my back, very still, uncomfortably until Ron took it off.

I sat up, and, with a flushed face and panic in my eyes, whispered: "Mom, I want to go home."

There were really only two times in my young life when I wished in my heart things could be different—that I was different—that *I* was normal.

The first time was that day in Ron's office when I had to wear *that* contraption.

Chapter 3

Mom says my very first word was Zac. I was about two when my mouth curved around the name of our pet poodle, and, pointing to my chest to indicate that he was mine, declared: "Sac! Ssssac!"

Sadly, Zac felt otherwise. And in the end, Zac and I didn't get along because neither of us wanted to share our toys with the other. The only time Zac and I got along was during story-time, right before bed, when my mother would read us *Goldilocks and the Three Bears* or *Home for a Bunny* and Zac would lay curled up on the floor, sleeping.

It was a few months after I turned four, however, when Mom broke the news: first, that it would be better for Zac if he lived somewhere else, with another family who would pay more attention to him. Then, that our family of three—Mom, Dad and me—was about to get bigger, and not because of the arrival of another pet. Mom sat me down on the couch, ruffled my hair, and said she was three months pregnant. I looked at her wide-eyed. For starters I didn't know what pregnant meant. So Mom explained by taking my left hand and placing it on her stomach. "There is a baby inside," she whispered. "Your sister or brother!"

Mom says I just tilted my head to the side, shrugged and went back to watching *Sesame Street*. Then, as Mom's stomach kept getting bigger, she kept reminding me. She'd ask: "Spencer, you are going to be a big brother soon. What do you think we should name the baby?"

One day, I finally spoke up: "If it's a boy, let's name him Robin. If it's a girl, we can call her Pinhead." I had resolved that if I was going to have a younger sibling, it *had* to be a boy. He had to be Robin, to my Batman, of course!

Mom laughed and shook her head. "You are such a smart alec," she said. "You sure take after your Dad's side of the family." Grandpa West, my Dad and my Dad's brothers are all funny and fast with comebacks. Well, they *try* anyway.

When the baby's debut into the world neared, I went to stay with my Mom's sister, Diana, who lived around the block from us. Normally, I didn't like being away from my parents, but I loved going to Aunt Diana's house. She would let me build big forts in her living room, using cushions from her couch and unused sheets from the hall closet. My Mom didn't let me build such monumental forts in my own home.

Typically, I would have stayed with Grandma and Grandpa Callas, as I loved sleepovers at their house. Grandma Callas would be at my beck and call, and was always feeding me delicious treats like potica cookies, homemade caramel corn that we would pop together and cheese and crackers with Sprite to wash it all down. At night, she would let me take all of my snacks into the family room, which was in the basement, and we would watch grown-up shows together, like, *Designing Women, The Cosby Show* and her favorite program, *The Golden Girls*. Grandma Callas would scrub my back in the bath, which she prepared with bubbles that would be taller than me. Grandpa Callas even carried me into church on Sundays, down the aisle to the front pew, fearing that if I sat at the back I wouldn't see the priest.

But when the new baby was due to be born, Grandpa Callas was busy working as a policeman and Grandma Callas had opened a real estate agency, Callas Realty. Diana opened her arms to have me stay with her, so that I wouldn't be underfoot when the baby arrived.

It wasn't Robin. *It* was a girl. My sister Annie was the new addition to our family. Right away, Diana and I went to see the baby for ourselves.

Once inside Mom's hospital room, I pulled myself up on her bed. First and foremost, I wanted a kiss, even though I had only been away from her for a day. Then I wanted to see this new child—who they had named Annie, not Pinhead! As Dad passed her to me, wrapped in a pink blanket, something happened which I didn't expect. When I looked into Annie's soft, brown eyes, I knew I was going to love having a sister. Annie was so cute with her dark brown hair and button nose. This was probably one of the first times, other than with my parents, that I felt true love.

Dad stood over me as I held Annie in my arms. She made gurgling sounds with her mouth and she seemed to be looking, well, nowhere. I learned when I was older that babies can't really see very much in front of them when they are first born, so while I saw Annie, she didn't see me. *Well*, I thought to myself, *she's not Robin, but I suppose Batgirl will do instead!*

For the most part, having another kid in the house was fine with me. I still got to watch *Sesame Street*, play outside and read with Mom and Dad at night. The one thing that did change after Annie was born was my bedroom. My room had always been upstairs right next to my parents' room. But Annie needed to be close to Mom, especially at night, if she woke up wanting to nurse. So my parents fixed up the basement— all for me.

During the day, it was great. I had the largest space in the house to play with my Superman, Batman and He-Man figurines. And yes, my Barbies—I was a boy who liked to play with dolls, too. But, like so many other kids, when the lights were turned off at night, that room became a playground for the monsters of my imagination. I spent many, many nights wide awake, eventually gaining the courage to climb down from my bed and scamper up the stairs as fast as my arms would carry me, en route to Mom and Dad's room, where I'd slip underneath the covers with them. During the day, I was a fearless superhero. At night, I was just plain scared.

As Annie and I started to get older, we began to have what my favorite comedian Dane Cook calls "nothing fights." Fights over absolutely nothing. Fights initiated by one of us, to push the other's buttons—it's just what siblings do, I guess. In the beginning, it was easy for me, as I was older and bigger. When the fights turned into hair pulling, pinching and throwing things at each other, Mom would step in. "Spencer," she would say, shaking a finger at me. "You need to watch what you are doing with Annie. One day she is going to be bigger than you. And on that day, I can assure you, she will get you back." And just as my Mom predicted, Annie got me back. One house rule that Dad came up with very early on was: "Annie, no kicking. Spencer can't kick back!" Annie liked to attack me physically, while I just spouted insults.

I was always conscious that I was smaller than my sister and all of my friends. But I didn't care. I loved being short. And it definitely had its advantages—I was the champ of hide and go seek and dodgeball, for example.

Now let's go back to that contraption that Mom, Dad and I ended up just calling "the brace." Mom would slip it on before bed. But as soon as the lights were out I'd spend the next ten minutes or so undoing the buckles and lifting myself out of it again. Sometimes, to make Mom happy, I would wear the brace for a few hours before removing it. All the while, I would lay there staring at the ceiling, barely able to roll over.

For a year, Mom and I pretended. I pretended I was trying to wear the brace and Mom pretended I was doing an OK job at it. But a year is a long time to pretend. The truth is, we both quietly gave up.

Dr. Coleman knew when we showed up for my one-year check-up.

"Nothing has changed," he exclaimed, throwing his hands in the air. "Nothing at all!"

"Well," Mom started, "I know he is not wearing it at night to bed. But he does wear it around the house to make up for the night hours he's missing."

"I understand," Dr. Coleman said, studying the X-rays. "But I do not think this is the best course of treatment after all. His leg bones are just not straightening. My worst fear was that this wouldn't work. And it's not."

My Mom shook her head. "Doctor, he doesn't want to wear it. Is there something else we can do? Is there not some other course of treatment?"

"I think so. But it will involve amputating far more of his legs."

"Oh."

Dr. Coleman then explained his alternate plan, which was to amputate my legs just below the pelvis bone. Unfortunately, to use prosthetics, he said, doctors like as much of the existing muscle and bone as possible to be there. "But in Spencer's case, he can't wear the prosthetic legs when his bones are at such an awkward angle. We want to see Spencer walk. And perhaps we still can help him walk, but it will be more challenging."

"I'm not sure Spencer wants to walk," Mom replied.

"He might not, and that's OK," Dr. Coleman said. "This boy certainly gets around just fine on his own anyway."

I had got my way with the brace, and I was getting my way with everything else, too. Mom would let me play outside in the rain, splashing in the puddles and dancing like I was Little Orphan Annie, shouting, at the top of my lungs, "The sun will come out, tomorrow, bet your bottom dollar that tomorrow, there'll be sun!" Mom didn't even bat an eyelash when I'd hop into my fire-engine-red toy car and go barrelling down the driveway at top speed, just managing to turn the wheel onto the sidewalk in time, before racing out into the street.

"You know, Tonette," I overheard Grandma Callas say one Sunday night after a big family dinner at our house. "I worry about Spencer. Aren't you afraid he's going to get hurt running around the way he does?"

I was in the living room, watching television with Annie, who was sitting beside me on the couch.

"Mom, I've told you before, kids will be kids. And Spencer doesn't want to be any different from the other kids," replied Mom.

There was a long pause. I heard Mom begin to clear up the plates and wine glasses. "Besides," I heard her say with a sigh. "What if something happens to Kenny and I? I know you, Dad or Jamie would look after Spencer and Annie. But I don't want to raise Spencer to be dependent on anyone. If we do everything for Spencer, then he will begin to think he's different and he won't learn to look after himself. He won't learn to take the risks he needs to take in life. And he won't become his own person."

"OK, Tonette," Grandma Callas replied. "Well, I'm going to

continue to spoil him no matter."

My mother laughed. "Of course, Mom."

My fifth birthday wasn't a happy one. Sure, I got a homemade cake shaped like a sailboat, decorated in gooey brown and white icing with Life Savers candies as the life preservers. And yes, the presents piled in: a He-Man sword and shield, a Rainbow Brite doll and a My Little Pony.

But I also knew another surgery was coming up.

Mom and Dad sat me down to explain that since I wasn't wearing the brace anymore, the doctors were going to remove even more of my legs in a few months. I gulped. This time things were different; I knew what to expect and truly understood what was happening. I didn't care that I was losing my legs—that was the good part, as it would be so much easier for me to get around on my hands without dragging "what's left" of my legs behind me. Not to mention that the last time I was in the hospital I got some pretty sweet gifts. This time I was hoping for a Teddy Ruxpin, an animated teddy bear that would tell you stories and his mouth actually moved. (Hey, don't judge, it was the '80s!) What I was terrified about was sleeping alone in a strange place and strange bed surrounded by other sick kids. It's a hollow feeling unlike any other, and, by far, more painful than losing my legs.

Soon, after the surgery, it was my very first day of school ever—I was so excited. Up until then, Mom had been teaching me to read phonetically: *Aaaa* is apple. *Beee* is Batman.

Ssss is Superman. And *Zzzz* for Zac! But I couldn't read any words—I just recognized letters from the books that were now piling up in my bedroom—from the Berenstain Bears collection to Disney classics like *Pinocchio* and *Cinderella*. I mostly wanted to go to school to learn to read them.

I woke up an hour early on that September day in 1986, and donned a pair of black shorts, a white button-up shirt and a navy blue V-neck sweater. I looked over at my Batman costume and its cape, hanging in my closet, and started to put that on, too. Then I changed my mind. (I didn't want people to know my secret identity on the first day. That could always wait until the second day.) I walked down the hall on my hands to the kitchen where Mom was waiting with my breakfast of her delicious cinnamon toast, which was my favorite. Mom sat down at the table with me and after she'd had a few sips of coffee, she turned to me and asked, "School starts today. Are you excited?"

I smiled and nodded. "Let's go, Mom," I said, hopping down off the bright yellow chairs at the small table in the kitchen where we often ate breakfast and lunch.

"Hold on, Spence," she replied. "Let's get your backpack and make sure you've got everything you need for the day." My Mom was, and still is, extremely organized.

Mom and I had driven past Overland Elementary School, which was located a few blocks from my house, a thousand times. I had pushed myself on my skateboard to the school playground a thousand times more, through the small walkway in between two houses, which was a shortcut to the school's swings, jungle gym and slides. But as we pulled up, my stomach started to churn. I felt uneasy. I was suddenly not so sure about school anymore. *I'll be on my own*, I thought to myself. *Will the students even like me? Or will they point and ask questions like so many other kids did? Will the teachers like me? Would we get snacks?* All of these questions popped into my head as Mom parked the car.

I stayed frozen in my seat as Mom got out and walked around to the trunk of our Cadillac. She got out my walker and my new prosthetic legs. I had had my second surgery in May. Now, only about three inches of the top parts of my legs remained. The surgery itself wasn't painful. I recovered quickly and was manoeuvring around the house within a few months, just like I had before. The only pain I felt was when Mom and Dad left the hospital. Like when I had my first surgery, I was awake for hours that night, listening to the children in my ward crying for their own mothers and fathers. I hugged my stuffed animal, Dumbo, close to me and waited for morning and the chance to go home. The same feeling was starting to bubble to the surface—there was nothing I could do to control it.

For the past few months at home, I had been using the prosthetic legs and the walker, mostly around the house, to practise for using them at school.

Mom opened the passenger side door. She then indicated for me to undo my seat belt and spin around. I wanted to protest, to tell Mom that I refused to wear the prosthetic legs on my first day of school—those ugly metal things, with foam in the middle, similar to the pair I first shuddered at when I saw them hanging on the wall at Intermountain Limb and Brace. "Those won't be my legs," I had said. But they were. My "starter legs," as Ron called them, were not the fancy, almost real-looking legs, with soft, skin-colored foam. Rather, in these—I felt like a freak. Like everyone would be staring at me.

I wanted to enter the school like the swarm of other students, carrying bright colored backpacks and skipping alongside their parents.

"Mom," I said, my eyes circling the other students. "Do I have to?" Mom followed my gaze. She understood.

"No," she whispered, while Annie happily sat in her car seat in the back. Mom had taken a part-time job at a daycare, which allowed her to bring Annie. Mom helped look after twenty children—reading, doing arts and crafts, and singing songs. The plan was that she would work half a day at the daycare, located on the other side of town, and then pick me up when school finished.

I smiled and hopped out of the car, landing softly on my hands. Mom put the legs away.

I walked on my hands through the parking lot and into the foyer of the school. Judy, who would be my physiotherapist for the first two years until a woman named Susan took over, immediately greeted me. Mom spoke with her and it was agreed that I would only wear the prosthetic legs during my time with Judy. All other times, I would get around on my hands, my usual, more comfortable way.

"Spencer just wants to fit in," I heard Mom tell her.

Cheryl, our backyard neighbor, came running out of the office and gave me a big hug. Cheryl and Judy, Mom had told me about a week earlier, would be helping me at school, mostly in learning to use my legs and the walker. I had never met Judy before, and while Cheryl lived right behind me, I had only met her a few times. She had shoulder-length blonde hair, bright blue eyes and a big, wide smile. Whenever she was outside in her backyard, barbecuing or working in her garden, she would wave for me to come over. I never did. I was very shy around people, particularly adults I didn't know. I think it all started when I was little and grown-ups would peer into my stroller and then shudder, asking Mom what was wrong with me. While I may not have actual memories of this, intuitively I think it has affected me. I do remember a time when I was about seven-years-old that a friend of Mom's had become disabled following a motorcycle accident. We were at the county fair. A small kid bolted over to us and just *stared*. Didn't say anything to us, just openly gazed at us. That was the second time in my life I wished I had been born with legs that worked. I would have run right over to this kid and told him to get lost, to be truthful.

Judy and I made our way down the hallway of the single-storey school, past the empty bulletin boards and bare walls waiting for future paintings and spelling tests to be posted, to a sunny, yellow-painted classroom at the very back of the school.

I sat in the doorway, looked around and shuddered. Some of the other kids had arrived and were seated on the floor, while the teacher, Mrs. Paul, in a beautiful floral cotton dress, sat in a chair facing everyone.

"You must be Spencer," Mrs. Paul piped up when she saw me. "Come and sit down," she continued in a soft voice, her hand gesturing for me to join the others on the floor.

I plopped myself down beside a boy with dark curly hair.

"I'm Matthew," he turned and said to me with a great grin.

"I... I... I am Spencer," I stuttered, wringing my perspiring hands together.

"Look what I have," he said, pulling out some small superhero figurines from his front pocket. "My favorite is Spider-Man. Here, you take this one." Matthew handed me Batman.

I smiled. I was going to enjoy kindergarten.

Not surprisingly, Matthew and I became close friends. Until he and his family left Rock Springs two years later, we were inseparable. Our group of two almost immediately widened to include a blonde girl named Amber and a girl with dark brown hair named Jenae.

It was only a matter of months into kindergarten when I began doing whatever I could to shorten the designated times I would spend with Judy or Cheryl learning to use the legs. I would fall behind in the hallway, after they picked me up at the classroom, so we would arrive late to their office. Once there, I would come up with some story or other that I just had to share with them. Like how Matthew had lost his first tooth biting into an apple, or how I had read my first book. But it was no use. Judy or Cheryl would make me speed things up, so they could spend the entire elected time with me wearing the legs.

Why didn't I like the fake legs? Physically, they were painful. They rubbed against me and chafed my skin. They were big and bulky and slowed me down. I had mastered getting around using my hands as my feet. I felt I was just like any other kid when I got around in that way; not having legs didn't hold me back from sliding and climbing at the playground. But when I wore the prosthetic legs, I felt different. I once asked my Mom: "People know that I don't have legs, so why are the doctors trying to trick people into believing I do?" She shook her head and replied, simply, "Just try." I didn't understand. To me, the legs were a lie.

Back at home at the end of the day, as the music of Barbara Streisand and the aromas of oregano and garlic from Italian cooking filled our house, Mom would often ask, "Did you use your walker and legs today?"

"Yes! Absolutely!" I'd reply. "I used them for, hmmm ... I think ten minutes. Maybe twenty."

"Spence," Mom would sigh. "You have to try harder, please."

"Sure, Mom," I'd say, nodding.

And I did try. Much in the same way I tried with the brace, which I guess wasn't very hard. Whenever I visited the Shriners Hospital for my check-ups, I would have to show Ron and now Dr. Lamb who had taken over for Dr. Coleman, and Barbara, the prosthetic clinic coordinator, how I walked with the legs.

"You know, Spencer," Ron would say. "If you'd use your legs more, if you really got used to wearing these all the time, I would make you a pair of better legs, like these," he'd say pointing to the fancy skin-like models I wanted from the beginning. "But these cost big bucks to make. If you're not going to use them, the Shriners can't spend the money."

Aside from the times I had to use the walker and the legs, I *loved* school. I excelled at nearly every subject, but especially English and music. In Grade 4, I started taking piano lessons. I worked my way quickly through "Twinkle, Twinkle, Little Star" and "Mary Had a Little Lamb" to "The Entertainer."

I also loved our field trips, when we would pile into buses, sing songs and bump along the dusty country roads of southern Wyoming. In the early grades, my class would go to a local farm every spring. In the winter of Grade 3, my entire class went ice skating at the Recreation Center. I tied a pair of children's skates onto my hands and, wearing a hockey helmet, slid along the ice, effortlessly. I may not have been as fast as the other kids, but I didn't care. I was just happy to be there, gliding along. When Amber and Jenae could skate as well as me, we would skate beside each other circling the rink, sometimes for an entire afternoon. No one thought it was strange, either. I was just, well, Spencer, the kid with no legs—who could ice skate.

In the later grades, the field trips got more serious. Southern Wyoming has a rich history and is known for a few things—including the Pony Express. From 1860 to 1861, a relay of riders on thoroughbred horses and mustangs ferried mail service from the eastern to the western U.S. They connected our country at a time when it needed connecting: on the eve of the U.S. Civil War.

In Grade 4, our class went north, about an hour and a half, to the sleepy ghost town of South Pass, which, during the days of the Pony Express, was a bustling town where riders often rested for a night or two. South Pass wasn't just a stopping point for the Pony Express, however. It was also a key town in the Oregon Trail, the two-thousand-mile route that took settlers westward.

The town really evoked the Old West, and the trip there had a strong impression on me. Wind whistled through the broken glass windows. Tumbleweed flew past me as I walked on my hands down the dusty main street. Inside the abandoned saloon, where the Pony Express riders and pioneers would have sipped whisky and listened to the piano, I wondered if I would have survived. Life was tough back then. Many able-bodied migrants, let alone athletic Pony Express riders, died en route from the east coast to the west. Mostly, they died from diseases like pneumonia or malnutrition.

I walked the boardwalk to a one-room schoolhouse, located at the far end of town. Like the other buildings in the town, the windows were all broken, the floorboards creaked and there was a small hole in the roof. The children's small wooden desks, however, were intact and faced the teacher's desk, in the middle of which was a rusted old metal bell, which the teacher would have used to call the students into class after recess. So this is where I would have gone to school, I mused.

The following year, our class recreated an 1800s pioneer town on the Oregon Trail. My friends and I dressed up in outfits the pioneer children would have worn, including billowy tops, rough cotton trousers and long flowered dresses, with aprons and hats, for the girls. The teachers called it Frontier Day.

"Between 1841 and 1869, more than a quarter of a million people headed across America," one of the teachers told us at an assembly before we traveled as a school en masse out onto the trail. "They did so following a few trails, which the Pony Express often criss-crossed. The most famous was the California Trail. Another, which diverted at various places, including at South Pass, was the Oregon Trail."

The night before, Grandma West had told me over our Sunday family dinner that gold partly fuelled the mass migration. Also sparking part of the exodus was the concept of Manifest Destiny—that it was God's will and the right of all Americans to expand westward. "We Mormons," Grandma West said, "were a good example of this." She and Grandpa West belonged to the Mormon Church, although neither went on a regular basis. They were familiar with the history and the struggles of the Mormons as they came to settle in Wyoming and Salt Lake City.

"But Spence," Grandma West laughed when I began to ask her more questions about Joseph Smith. "Just enjoy churning butter and the square dancing. Leave all this religious history talk to another day."

We did make butter on Frontier Day—creamy, salty butter that I smothered on homemade sourdough bread and crackers.

Hollywood and television depicts the greatest risk to the pioneers as the American Indians. But truth be told, as I learned on Frontier Day, the weather—from thunderstorms to torrential rains to temperatures of minus thirty degrees (like we sometimes get in midwinter in Wyoming)—was the early settlers' main opponent. Many died trying to make it to California.

"If they managed to make it all the way to the west coast, the settlers would say 'we've seen the elephant,'" explained one of our teachers. "We made it all the way through the canyons, the Rockies, through the desert plains and the snow! Those who turned back, as many did, would say they saw the elephant's tail."

In Grade 5, my class actually followed part of the Oregon Trail, leaving the school first thing in the morning and hiking to White Mountain, about a two-hour walk. I sat in a wooden hand-pulled cart, similar to what pioneers used. Jennifer, a girl in my class, had hurt her ankle and sat beside me as some of the stronger kids pulled us up the slope. We weighed too much and a wheel broke halfway up the mountain, but we eventually made it after my teacher, Mr. Pribyl, mended the broken wheel. We rested at the waterfall located behind White Mountain, where we had a pioneer meal of chicken and rice, cooked by some of the parents, followed by peach cobbler.

As I made my way through elementary school, I fell even more in love with Wyoming. While I don't think I would have wanted to be alive then, I came to appreciate our rich heritage—the role this windy state played in creating America and our multicultural society.

Essentially, and despite not having any legs, I was just like any other kid. I was a Boy Scout from Grade 3 until Grade 6. My first of many appearances in our local newspaper, the *Daily Rocket-Miner*, was a photograph of my troop and me collecting trash. I was also proud to sing Rod Stewart's "Forever Young" at Aunt Jamie's wedding to Uncle Phillip. And in Grade 4, Dad and I entered and won the Pinewood Derby, a race involving twelve-inch wooden cars that competitors had to build from scratch. Dad and I spent hours in the garage, gluing wood and measuring weights. But in the end, we had a sleek royal blue Pinewood car with a yellow strip down the middle and a big, glistening trophy that I still have to this day. Like I said, normal American kid.

The only thing that *did* make me feel different were the fake legs and walker. In Grade 2, my parents had sensed I was still having difficulty adjusting to the legs, so they bought me a wheelchair. Both were worried that using my arms as if they were legs and my hands as if they were feet might cause stress on my body over time. "What happens if you pull a muscle?" my Mom asked. "And besides, you can't get everywhere on your prosthetic legs," she told me.

But I can get everywhere with the use of my hands and arms—and I never get tired. I will never pull a muscle, I thought.

But all the people helping me, from Dr. Lamb to Susan and Cheryl, were so proud when I walked that I didn't often voice my dislike for the legs. As soon as I was done with my exercises, though, I would discard the equipment, opting to use the wheelchair and my hands to get around.

Occasionally, I made jokes about the legs, like the time Cheryl plucked me out of class early for my practice session. She needed to drop something off at the office. I, of course, was slow and fell behind. "Spencer, I've got things to do today," Cheryl said. "Will you shake a leg?"

As soon as she said this, she stopped and stared at me red-faced. Before she could say anything, however, I lifted one of my prosthetic legs and shook it.

"Like this?" I replied, laughing.

"I am so sorry," Cheryl said, running up to me and giving me a big hug. "Sometimes my mouth opens and things pop out, even when my head is saying stop!"

We both laughed so hard we didn't hear the bell. We were still laughing in the middle of the hall when the students rushed out of their classrooms, nearly trampling us en route to the lunchroom.

Dr. Lamb and Ron weren't laughing, though, when I saw them during my regular three-month check-ups. In fact, they didn't even crack a smile.

"You need to do more," Dr. Lamb would lecture my Mom and Dad. Even in Grade 4, when I discarded the walker for crutches, Dr. Lamb seemed only semi-impressed. "It's great that he is using crutches but you need to encourage him to wear the legs everywhere he goes," he told my parents.

"I understand, but Spencer doesn't like them," my Mom would reply. "He is fine getting around without the legs and crutches. He uses his hands."

During another check-up, Dr. Lamb pressed on: "Every child wants to walk. Are you telling me Spencer doesn't?"

"I don't know what Spencer wants," Mom sighed. "He will say he's happy using the crutches. Then I'll turn around and he'll be scooting out the door on his hands. Spencer isn't the type of child who complains. I gauge his needs and wants from his actions. And I don't think he likes his prosthetic legs."

"How is he integrating with the other children if he isn't walking?" Barbara asked. "Is he falling behind in school?"

"He has straight-A grades," Mom replied. "And, he has a wide circle of friends—he's always out and about with them."

"Oh," Barbara hummed, her eyes downcast.

One lunch hour, near the end of Grade 6, Susan, Cheryl, my Mom and I made the decision to abandon the legs and crutches altogether. We were gathered around a table in the staff room of Overland Elementary, discussing the challenges I would face once I graduated and headed off to White Mountain Junior High. Starting in Grade 7, every period I would have to switch rooms. I wouldn't have the same desk all day long, in which I could store all my books, pens and papers. I would have to carry these items in a backpack. I would also have to use a locker and traverse the long, narrow hallways of junior high, which had a population of well over seven hundred. Compared to Overland, which had about three hundred students, it was huge.

"It could be dangerous for Spencer," Cheryl said, shaking her head. "All it would take is one child bumping up against him and *boom!* Down he goes! Like that time in the second grade." Robbie, an older student, had rushed past me and accidentally tripped me. It was in the entranceway to the school and I fell on some ceramic tile, face first.

"You had a goose egg on your head the size of a baseball," Mom added.

"And two black eyes," Cheryl said.

Mom looked at me and asked: "Spencer, do you really want to give up your legs?"

All of my friends—for that matter, all of Rock Springs—accepted me the way I was. It was those gawky horrible legs that made me feel like I didn't belong. Pretending to be something I wasn't, a child who could walk, was what made me feel I stood out.

"Yes, Mom," I nodded, enthusiastically. "Yes, yes, yes please!"

So long fake legs.

On my last day of Grade 6, I had a goodbye lunch with Cheryl. We sat under a cottonwood tree, feasting on sandwiches and, of course, Scotch-a-Roos—peanut butter, butterscotch and chocolate Rice Krispies, which Cheryl loved to make. We reminisced about my time at Overland Elementary. Cheryl then gave me a beautiful quilt that she and all my teachers had worked on over the past year. Each square was different and represented that teacher's personal experience of having me as a student. (There was a picture of Batman, of course, courtesy of my third grade teacher.) To this day, the quilt hangs on a wall in my bedroom in Rock Springs.

At one point, Cheryl and I, sprawled out on our backs on top of the quilt, quietly stared up at the branches and leaves of the tree. I recalled a book our Grade 3 teacher had read to us by Wilson Rawls, called *Where the Red Fern Grows*. It is a story about a boy named Billy and his two Redbone Coonhounds, which die at the end of the book. (I know what you're thinking, how is the death of two dogs sentimental? Just stay with me on this one.) A part of the novel came to my mind on that day:

> Lying back in the soft hay, I folded my hands behind my head, closed my eyes and let my mind wander back over the two long years. I thought of the fishermen, the blackberry patches and the huckleberry hills. I thought of the prayer I had said when I asked God to help me get two hound pups. I knew He had surely helped, for He had given me the heart, courage and determination.

My Mom and Dad had decided early on to raise me in the Catholic Church. Grandpa and Grandma West and Dad were lapsed Mormons. So I attended Sts. Cyril and Methodius Church along with Mom, her sisters and her parents. I took my first communion in Grade 4. I was even a lector in Grade 6, reading sections from the Bible that the priest, Father Fred, chose for me.

Truth be told, I wasn't sure what I believed in. But I did pray. And on that day with Cheryl, under the cottonwood tree, I silently thanked whatever it was in the universe that had given me the good fortune to be alive.

Chapter 4

At the same time that I was learning about the history of Wyoming, my family was also telling me about, well, themselves. As Shirley Abbott said in *Womenfolks: Growing Up Down South*: "We all grow up with the weight of history on us. Our ancestors dwell in the attics of our brains as they do in the spiralling chains of knowledge hidden in every cell of our bodies." This quote really embodies the importance of family and knowing your personal history. Culture has always been a big part of our family and I loved listening to our family history. (The only stories I light-heartedly dreaded were my Dad's hunting and fishing stories, told again and again. Each story getting bigger and wilder every time he recited them. But that's family for you.)

This got me thinking about my own family and the threads that bound us together. I started not just listening intently to my family's stories, but also begging to learn more. I wanted to discover how I came to be confident, independent, cocky and artistic. I wanted to know about my ancestors and how a kid like me came to live in rural Wyoming.

In the years to come, I realized I wanted to learn as much about every member of my family as I could, and, like searching out puzzle pieces, discover the parts of them that went into making me.

The earliest person—or *character*, for every one of my ancestors danced to their own tunes—I learned about was my great-grandfather, Giovanni, who died before I was born. Giovanni Corona, Mom's maternal grandfather, was a tiny man, who, in his older years, liked to wear white short-sleeved shirts with billowy silk scarves and suspenders. Despite having lived in America for more than sixty-five years, he always spoke English with a thick European accent and wildly gesturing hands.

Giovanni was born and raised in Vinchiaturo, Italy. The Corona family was poor. Giovanni went to school in the same worn shoes and hand-me-down clothes for many years. His mother, Antonia, the matriarch, stayed home and watched over her family with a careful eye and broom, which she would smack on the bottom of any wayward child of hers.

Despite studying hard, getting good marks and rarely, if ever, skipping school to play street games with the other boys, Giovanni, in Antonia's eyes, was the most wayward of all her children. Giovanni, you see, wanted to be a professional musician. He wanted to play the accordion. Antonia thought that was foolish and forbade any instrument to pass by the threshold of the tiny, one-bedroom home. And she kept tabs on her son wherever he went, making sure he was not sneaking music lessons from the violinist who played by the fountain in the center of town. She was a tough matriarch, let me tell you.

I soon learned from whom my mother inherited her confidence. Her strength to discard what the doctors told her about my health and follow her own instincts instead, for nothing could stop Giovanni from pursuing his dream. In 1909, at the age of seventeen, Giovanni left Vinchiaturo. He boarded a ship at Naples, Italy, and headed straight for Ellis Island, New York City. To help him navigate his way from the ship through U.S. immigration services, an American customs officer in Italy pinned a piece of paper to the lapel of his grey wool jacket. On it was his immigration number and an anglicized version of his name: *John Corona*.

John stayed for a few years in New York. He then made his way north, to Canada, across the swaying grasslands of the Prairies to the hemlock, pine and cedar trees of the west coast of British Columbia. He stayed in Vancouver working to save money to buy a brand new Guerrini accordion. It was not a cheap instrument, and buying it left him little money to pay for accordion lessons. By and large, John taught himself how to play.

After a few years in Vancouver, he headed southeast to Butte, Montana, where he worked in the copper mines and started playing the accordion for anyone who would listen. Word started to get around that John was talented and people slowly started hiring him to play at anniversaries and weddings.

When John wasn't playing the accordion or working, he played cards with the other immigrants in the mining camp where he lived. They were all slowly learning English, mostly from conversations with their supervisors. Around the card table, men from Yugoslavia, Poland and Germany would nod, grumble in their native languages and then cheer wildly when they won a hand or snarl at each other when they lost. Likely names were slung around the table. But the mining camps were places where men connected more than they fought. After all, they shared a common bond—they were each alone in a strange country.

Then John heard through the grapevine about an accordion-playing contest. He decided to enter and won first place. The prize was a beautiful diamond ring. An agent signed John afterward and he quit his job at the copper mine to tour full-time. The six-month Vaudeville Company tour traveled the northwest United States and the Rocky Mountains.

One thing I have learned in life, and John eventually conceded, too, is that mothers are rarely wrong. (Frustrating, I know, but it's so true.) After just one year on the road, John grew tired of the long nights playing the accordion. He wanted a house, a wife and children to come home to every night. John knew there were jobs in coal mining in Wyoming, so he quit the touring part of the music business and took a full-time job as a coal miner with the Union Pacific Coal Company. He stayed with the company for nearly thirty years, taking only one long holiday, in 1929, to return to Vinchiaturo to find himself a wife.

Colomba, my great-grandmother, was a thin, slight woman sixteen years younger than John. The two first met when Colomba was just a baby, as their families were friends and lived in the same village. During his visit years later, John ran into Colomba in Vinchiaturo and fell in love. He then asked both his Dad and Colomba's Dad if he could marry her, and they were married soon thereafter. They stayed in Italy until March of 1930 and then John headed back to the United States with his new bride.

My grandma, Rosemary, was born on October 18, 1937, in Rock Springs. John took a day off at the coal mine to be present for her birth. He and Colomba lived in a small two-room shack, in an older part of Rock Springs where a number of immigrants lived. Not long after Rosemary's birth, the family (which already included Rosemary's older sister, Antonia, and her brother, Tony) moved to a larger house owned by John's employer. In 1945, the Union Pacific Coal Company sold that house to John for a thousand dollars. The house, which Rosemary would live in until her wedding day, didn't have an inside bathroom or hot running water. The family used a woodshed outhouse in the backyard and hot water from the kettle in the kitchen when they needed to bathe.

Not wanting to repeat the same mistakes as his mother, John taught Tony to play the accordion starting when he was a small child. In fact, John taught many Rock Springs children how to use the instrument. Tony, too, excelled at the accordion, winning local and district talent shows. As a teenager, he joined an orchestra that played at dances, weddings and anniversary parties. And not long after he graduated high school, Tony married his childhood sweetheart and moved to Colorado, where he got a job working for a wholesale musical instrument distributor. Later Tony started his own business, Tony Corona Wholesale, which distributed musical accessories such as guitar strings and harmonicas. When John died at age eighty-two from heart disease, likely a result of all the years breathing in coal dust while on the job, he bequeathed his prized diamond ring to Tony.

For my grandmother, life as a girl in the coal-mining camp was hard. (Maybe this is why she liked to coddle me; she didn't want me to endure the same trials and tribulations she had.) Those babies who had the misfortune of being born in the fall, as Rosemary was, had to struggle for survival through a cold, bitter winter during which temperatures often dipped to thirty degrees below zero. Most of the houses of the mining employees were made of wood or stone and heated by coal fires. Influenza and chicken pox made their way from one house to the other every year. Luckily, Rosemary survived that first risky winter.

In December of 1941, when Rosemary was only four, World War II came to the doorstep of the United States when the Japanese bombed Pearl Harbor. Grandma's memories of the war included ration stamps, issued by the government, which Colomba used to purchase scarce items like butter and sugar.

At the end of the war, Rosemary started school. Colomba and John spoke Italian in the home, so Rosemary enjoyed finally having English-speaking friends. During their play-dates, she and a small group of girls would have tea parties and sip imaginary lemonade from their mothers' chipped por-celain cups.

One thing the family did together was make wine, with grapes grown in California. Every fall, Rosemary, Antonia and Tony would slip off their sandals and, barefoot, jump on the grapes in big barrels in the backyard, squishing them into a pulp, which John would ferment in the garage. Many Rock Springs immigrant families made wine. It was a staple often referred to as Dago Red. Every Sunday, Rosemary's family would hold big dinners of roasted turkey, squash and marsh-mallows, pastas with homemade spaghetti sauces and fresh-baked apple pies.

Now my grandfather, Jim Callas, who would become Rose-mary's husband, was also born in a coal-mining camp, in Helper, Utah, to immigrant parents. His father, Bill, was born in Crete, Greece, and came to the United States at age seven-teen just like John. He took a steam train across the northern states and he eventually landed in Kemmerer, Wyoming. Bill wasn't pursuing any dream of becoming a musician, though, or escaping a domineering mother. He just wanted a job, and they were hard to come by in Crete. He went to work in the coal mines, became an American citizen and then, in 1918, joined the U.S. Army.

No one in the family is quite sure where Bill and his wife, Joan Ricardo, met or when they married. But they eventually moved to Helper, Utah, where they had five children: Bill Jr.,

John, Phyllis, Jim and Tom.

Helper wasn't that far from Rock Springs—five hours by car in the 1930s. Rock Springs had many coal mines, while Helper was beginning to shut down some of its shafts. Worrying that he might soon be jobless, Bill moved to Rock Springs in 1941. Once he was settled with a good job, he returned to Helper to get his family. Joan, however, wouldn't leave, so Bill headed to Wyoming with all five children.

Bill worked three different shifts in the coal mines to support his family as a single Dad. And in his off hours, he loved to cook. And he was mighty good—homemade bread and crispy biscuits, delicious cakes and rabbit stew. He raised rabbits and chickens right in the backyard of the family's tiny two-bedroom home. Yet Bill was also determined to be one of the first on the street to install indoor plumbing and a toilet.

Phyllis grew tired of living in a house full of men and moved back to Helper to be with her mother. Bill and Joan drifted apart, and eventually divorced. Bill took custody of the boys, while Joan remained in Helper with her daughter.

My grandfather, Jim, attended Superior High School in Superior, Wyoming, while Rosemary went to Rock Springs High School. (Just like Mom and Dad later would, and then eventually me). Jim and Rosemary never met in their teen years. Jim and his brothers excelled in every sport they played, but Jim never got a chance to know what it would be like to be a star basketball player. He quit early to join the U.S. Air Force, which was fighting in Korea. He worked as a mechanic.

Jim was stationed at the Weathersfield Royal Air Force Station in England with the 20th Fighter Bomber Wing for nearly a year and a half. He worked hard and he only ever took one holiday. It was with his father, who, in 1952, was traveling through London to Crete to marry his second wife, Annie, a young village girl.

While the population of Rock Springs was, and still is, small, there were enough immigrants back then, working in the coal mines, to support a Greek Orthodox Church. The church's priest, a large man who wore a long black robe and liked to fill his church with incense imported from the Mediterranean, did some matchmaking on the side.

Annie's picture had been sent to the priest with a letter from her father saying she wanted to marry a nice Greek man and move to America. The priest intended to pass on the letter to a young man who had just arrived from Athens. But Great-grandpa Callas was there when the priest took a knife and carefully opened the wax-sealed envelope. Bill took one look at the black and white photograph of Annie, who had long dark hair and soft eyes, and declared: "I'm going to Greece by the end of the week. I'll bring her here, as my wife!"

Annie and Bill were married in Greece in 1955. They returned to the United States and had a child, Goldie, a dark-haired girl with an angelic face like her mother's. Bill died in 1967 from liver disease. After, Annie and Goldie moved to Salt Lake City, Utah, where they both still live.

When Jim finished his tour of duty in the air force, he returned to Rock Springs and took a job as an electrician's assistant for Union Pacific Railroad. A friend of Jim's introduced him to Rosemary and the two hit it off right away. Jim, like his Dad had, often worked nights. Rosemary would make him dinner, which she would bring to his work in a wicker basket.

Jim and Rosemary were married seven months after they began dating in Sts. Cyril and Methodius Church—the same church where I would attend Sunday school. At the reception, John and Tony played the accordion, while Annie and baby Goldie danced. There were Italian pastas and Greek *spanakopita*, roast beef and mashed potatoes. Everyone left in the wee hours of the morning, light-headed from John's famous wine.

As my grandmother Rosemary says of her one and only husband of fifty-three years: "Jim was not part of the Holy Rollers of Rock Springs." As in, the goodie-two-shoe kids who studied hard, played their sports even harder and attended church on a regular basis—the predominant faiths in Rock Springs being Catholic and Mormon.

"Jim was a greaser," Rosemary told me recently, as my grandfather stifled a laugh. "He and his brothers paraded around town in tight T-shirts, with cigarette packages bulging from their sleeves." Rosemary once showed up at Jim's work, with her usual picnic basket of goodies, to discover his Levi's ripped along the inner left seam. Rosemary scurried off to find a needle and thread only to return to find that Jim had fixed his pants with the office stapler.

Yet Rosemary knew that Jim could settle down. And he did.

He actually started back in high school, when he wanted to join the basketball team. The coach would have nothing to do with him unless he quit smoking. But just to show how serious Wyoming schools take their sports, some parents of the other members of the basketball squad, envious of Jim's natural sports ability, told the coach he was smoking, when he did, in fact, quit. Jim was kicked off the team and never played school sports again.

Jim also started to settle down when he converted to Catholicism from the Greek Orthodox faith so he could marry Rosemary in the church where she was baptized. (Also where their daughter, Jamie, would later wed her childhood sweetheart, Phillip, and where I would one day be a lector). It wasn't that Jim found God in the Catholic Church. But converting for the woman he loved was a sign that he was starting to take his life more seriously.

Just short of a year following Jim and Rosemary's nuptials, their bouncing baby daughter, Tammy, arrived. A year later Diana came screaming into the world. And a year and a half after that, Tonette, my mother, graced Jim and Rosemary with her gentle presence. Like my Dad, Jim had hoped that every one of his children would be a boy, someone he could groom into the next all-star basketball player for the Rock Springs Tigers. But when Jamie was born four years after Tonette, Rosemary packed up the baby-blue bonnet, matching booties and blanket that her sister had knitted for her and took the box to the Catholic Church, where the priest handed it over to a charity.

It didn't take long for that houseful of women to tame Jim for good. For one, the bills started to pile up. Heating, electricity, car payments, house payments, telephone, television and lots of mouths to feed. Jim took on a steady stream of work to keep on top of things—often juggling two or three jobs at a time. He drove fuel trucks for Grandpa West's company, Desert Oil, long before my Mom and Dad ever met. He also owned a drywall business and was a salesman for a wholesale food company.

After they were married, Jim and Rosemary bought a small three-bedroom, two-storey house on a quiet street. My mother shared a room with her sister Diana, while Tammy, who saw how hard her parents were working to take care of the family, volunteered to sleep beside and watch over her youngest sister, Jamie. But as Jamie aged, it was clear the family needed to move.

To buy a new house, Jim needed a stable job that would give him a big enough salary so he could start saving money. Simply, he needed a profession. Then, one rainy evening, as he was coming out of the supermarket to drop off groceries at home before heading to his nighttime gig hanging drywall, a sign on the bulletin board caught his eye:

Rock Springs Police Force

Looking for new recruits

Physical and written examinations to take place.

Jim dropped the bags and ran to the cashier, who loaned him a pen and the back of a discarded receipt to write down the information. Two days later, wearing his church suit, a white shirt and a tie, he showed up at the police station located on the second floor of city hall to take the tests.

But the tests were canceled. Not enough Rock Springs men had signed up.

Jim, feeling disappointed, walked slowly and silently to his car. When he arrived at home, he told Rosemary that the only place left to find permanent work was the trona mine. Trona is a mineral mined in Rock Springs that is used in baking soda, glass and toothpaste.

Jim wasn't even on the job a week, however, when the clerk for Rock Springs called to say that the police were doing the tests again. Jim sighed and informed him it was too late, he had taken another job. But the police force wanted him so much that the police chief, Louis Muir, called the mining company, who agreed to let Jim attend. A week after that, Jim, in tan slacks with a navy blue stripe down the outside of each leg, a navy blue button-down shirt, a tie and a cap, was Rock Springs' newest police officer. On his belt hung a canister of mace, a flashlight, a nightstick and a gun.

Over our long Sunday dinners, Grandpa Callas would tell us stories about his policing days. "At the time I first joined the force," he would begin. "Rock Springs was a sleepy family town. There were very few murders." My grandfather's duties mostly involved issuing speeding citations, traffic violations and responding to emergency calls. "All of the families in Rock Springs slept with their windows open in the summer and their doors unlocked pretty much all year round," my grandfather would chuckle.

That all changed for a while in the 1970s, when a large power plant began construction outside Rock Springs. The company wanted to keep costs down and they did so by hiring anybody and everybody, at cheap, cheap wages. The only men who would usually agree to such low salaries were drifters, grifters and ex-cons.

Coinciding with the power plant construction was an oil boom. Oil had been found sixty miles southeast of Rock Springs near a town called Wamsutter, drawing even more men to the area. Men with dazed looks in their eyes, similar to the dazed looks of the men of the 1800s lured west by the gold rush. It seemed that every "single" man in America and every family man in need of an escape from his family and a desire for fast cash descended on Rock Springs.

"Within a few short years, Rock Springs went from Andy Griffith's Mayberry to Sin City—at least that's what CBS's *60 Minutes* called it when they profiled our seedy town," my grandfather would say. "Yes, indeed. *This* town was the original Sin City."

Jim, who worked his way up the ranks of the tiny police force pretty quickly, mostly due to his hard work and sense of duty, was sergeant in charge of the detective division at the tail end of the Sin City days. Eventually, the crime was cleaned up—especially after the U.S. government convened senate hearings on the situation in Rock Springs. Within a few years, the drifters and grifters were replaced by hardworking family men.

One of those hardworking families was Keith and Marjene West and their clan of five children, the middle of which was my Dad, Kenny. Marjene's side of the family were immigrants from Finland, lured to the U.S., like Jim and Rosemary's Dads, to earn stable salaries in the coal mines. Keith, whose family came from England, could trace his lineage all the way back to British royalty.

My grandpa's Dad, Owen West, had started a gas company called Desert Oil, which provided Rock Springs with a few pumps. When the oil boom of the 1970s hit, the company also sent gas and diesel fuel to the oil companies drilling in the fields. Owen had also founded a theater, the West Theater, in downtown Rock Springs, which showed all the latest Hollywood releases.

Kenny had three brothers—Chuck, Steve and Neil—and a younger sister, Jan. Their Dad had bought the family a large home on Virginia Street in the posh new subdivision that was near where Rock Springs High School stands today. Coincidentally, my grandfather helped build the school, when he was head of the school board. Like his father, Keith didn't sit still.

"Do your best," he would bellow at his boys. "And give it all you've got."

For most of the 1970s, Keith was chairman of the school board. And for most of the 1980s, after Rock Springs' Sin City days, he was mayor. His greatest pride as head of the small town was building a large recreation center, which included a hockey arena and swimming pool. He did all this while running the family gas company and still making time for his family. (And Reed always said I could inspire people, look at Keith!)

On hot summer days, Kenny and his brothers would often sit in their swimsuits, with towels in their hands, on the roof of their shed that overlooked their neighbors' pool, hoping for an invitation to swim. At the time, their neighbors were one of the few families to have a pool in their backyard.

Even though Kenny's family had a big house, it wasn't big enough that all the children could have their own rooms. Kenny shared his with Neil. And one April Fool's Day, when he was about nine, Kenny and his older brother Steve tied Neil to the bed with thick camping rope when he was sleeping. When Neil awoke, his screams could be heard all the way down the street. When Keith, red-faced and threatening to ground all of his sons until they were thirty, finally managed to cut Neil free, Neil had to deal with his clothes next. Kenny and Steve had turned all of his drawers upside down, so that when Neil pulled them open, the contents fell on the floor into a big pile.

My grandmother, Marjene, tried her best. She'd make her kids their favorite foods, including green Jell-O and meatloaf, in an attempt to pacify them. But eventually she'd throw her hands up in the air and walk away, saying: "I'll let your father deal with it."

Yet from a very young age, Keith instilled in his children a love and respect for the environment and wildlife. He taught them gun safety, basic survival skills, how to use a compass and, if they were lost, to always head downhill and follow the river to the main road. When each of his sons turned fourteen, he gave them a gun for hunting. He would then take his boys to hunt deer, elk and antelope. They would butcher and process the animals into hamburger, steaks, roasts, salami, sausage and jerky—providing meat for the whole family, sometimes for an entire year.

Kenny and his family spent much of their summers at a cabin in Pinedale, Wyoming, that Owen bought in 1950. The boys would tell each other horror stories in the middle of the night, and on rainy days they'd have showers in a hollowed-out pine tree that was about a hundred years old and had been struck by lightning on more than one occasion.

Growing up, I would do the same things with my sister Annie—but I didn't need to tell her any horror stories. Something as simple as the wind rustling through a crack in the cabin's wall would freak her out. It made my job a lot easier.

Now, most kids glamorize their mothers at some point or another in their lives—even I did (and I still do—my Mom is the best). But the truth about my mother, Tonette, is that while she was and *still is* very beautiful, she was also a magnet for trouble as a child. When she and her sisters would walk down the street in their pretty white Sunday school dresses with big red bows, a dog would inevitably jump up on Tonette and not the others. The dog, of course, would have just been in a mud puddle. As Tonette would try to wipe herself clean with a white handkerchief, her three sisters would laugh uncontrollably.

Tonette's older sisters liked to tease her. One day, Tonette decided she had had enough. In a paper shopping bag, she packed a few pairs of socks and clean underwear, a pair of jeans and a sweater and ran away. She got as far as the next block, where her father, doing his rounds in the patrol car, saw her. After driving her home, he made Tammy and Diana apologize.

Tonette, like me, did well in school, and for several years she also joined the choir. When she was performing, she could forget that she was awkward and just enjoy being in the moment. (Makes sense that I inherited my love for singing from my Mom.)

Tonette's new-found confidence prompted her to try out for cheerleading, and she surprised everyone who thought her too clumsy by making the team. Slowly, Tonette's awkwardness disappeared altogether and she grew into the attractive, dark-haired teenager who eventually got the attention of Rock Springs' star athlete: Kenny West. At age fifteen, Kenny had scouts from two colleges out to the baseball diamond watching him play. He was also the top point guard on the Rock Springs High School basketball team. Kenny, with his chiselled good looks and dark hair, was frequently the object of the cheerleaders' gossip. I don't think he really minded as even today he proclaims that he's the handsomest man in the world, otherwise than his son, of course.

By the time he was twenty-one, however, Kenny had abandoned the idea of a life in professional sports because it would mean he would have to leave Rock Springs. Instead, he began working for his Dad's company. Kenny, who had graduated from high school, would often return to his alma mater to watch a game on his evenings off. His gaze typically landed on Tonette, four years his junior. Tonette had blossomed into a dark-haired beauty, with a tall, slim frame. Her awkwardness, while still there, somehow disappeared as she waved her black and orange pom-poms on the Rock Springs High School basketball court and football field.

The summer after Tonette graduated high school and was now working, he got up the courage to ask her out on a date. She declined, however, because she hardly knew him. But Kenny wasn't going to let Tonette get away with saying no.

Every time Kenny would pass Tonette while driving in his truck to his job at Desert Oil, and she was on her way to her work as an operator for Mountain Bell phone company, he would wave and flash her a big smile. Tonette would blush. It took several conversations, but eventually the girlfriend of a friend of Kenny's talked Tonette into giving him a chance. And they were a perfect match.

Tonette and Kenny had two things in common that would prove to be linchpins in keeping them together. Neither ever wanted to leave Rock Springs like many of the town's young people did—Kenny liked the outdoor life, while Tonette wanted to be near her mother and sisters. And Kenny and Tonette both wanted children.

A year after their first date, they married in Jim and Rosemary's living room. Just as he had at Rosemary and Jim's wedding reception, my great-uncle Tony played the accordion. There was Greek *spanakopita*, homemade lasagne, cabbage rolls, local Italian sausage called Kronski's, potica, pizzelle cookies and, of course, cake. The only thing missing was John's wine, for he had died five years before. But Kenny would eventually learn John's formula for wine making from his father-in-law, Jim, and the two of them would revive the annual tradition.

And two years after Kenny and Tonette were married, I was born.

So this is my family. Loving, crazy, bold, eccentric and courageous. Adjectives that people would soon come to use to describe me—for better or worse.

In the quiet moments of my life, I'd often sit and think about my ancestors and how grateful I was to have been born into this family. One of the very first times I recall having done this was the day before I started junior high.

Chapter 5

On the early autumn morning of 1993, when I was set to start junior high, my hands shook as I did up the buttons on one of the new shirts Mom and I had bought in Salt Lake City. My stomach churned so much, I couldn't eat breakfast. I sat quietly in the kitchen, listening to the hum of the refrigerator while Mom fiddled in the kitchen making breakfast for Annie, who was starting Grade 3. Soon after, a lift-equipped school bus picked me up at my house and took me to White Mountain Junior High, where I made my way up the ramp to the front entrance, my black canvas backpack sitting on the floor rest of my wheelchair. I was more than nervous.

I stopped just inside the school and looked at the timetable I was given over the summer holidays. Then I found my way to room 109, for English class, which would be my first period for the entire semester. Along the hallways, I saw familiar faces from Overland Elementary and from all over Rock Springs, as students from half of the elementary schools in the town would go to White Mountain. But I didn't see any of my close friends. Even during lunch they were nowhere to be found. I had my brown-bagged meal of salami, pepperoni, cheese and crackers (we *were* Italian), sitting at a long table with kids I recognized from somewhere, but couldn't quite place.

I finally connected with my close Overland friends, including Amber and Jenae, after school, but it was only a matter of weeks before we began to drift apart. In elementary school, it didn't matter that I was a boy and they were girls. We did everything together, from playing with dolls or Matchbox cars to water fights in the summer and sledding in the winter. But junior high brings with it a lot of changes, as I soon discovered. The girls began to whisper secrets to one another. Mostly, I learned later, they were talking about the cute boys on the football team. And Amber and Jenae soon found new friends, almost all girls.

Mom and Dad explained to me that growing apart from friends is part of life and that one day we might all come back together—and one day I would find new friends, too. "You're all changing, Spencer," Mom said. "You are young and just discovering who you are and what you like to do. You may find out you like different things, and that's OK. You'll find friends who are a better reflection of who you are."

Early on in junior high, I realized I was really interested in drama. I had enjoyed performing at piano recitals, at Aunt Jamie's wedding and at school concerts at Overland. And during the second week of the second semester of junior high, the head of the after-school theater club posted an announcement on the bulletin board in the foyer saying membership was open. The first meeting of the club would be in a week. Virginia, a girl in my Sunday school class, had been in the theater club the previous semester and she suggested I go to the meeting. "Spencer, you are always putting on voices and carrying on like you are an actor," she said. "I think you will love it!"

"Alrighty, then," I replied, imitating Jim Carrey in *Ace Ventura*.

Our first play at the theater club was *Empty Chairs,* set in an addiction rehabilitation center. I was a patient in the center. So was this girl with mousy blonde hair named Marci, who played the part of a boy with a crack cocaine addiction. Marci, without fail, always sat beside me at theater club, wanting to practise our lines together—I had one long monologue—and pestered me to hang out with her afterward. Marci wore sweatshirts, jeans and Converse running shoes. Her deep laugh filled the auditorium at White Mountain where the theater club met. I found Marci pushy and so different from Jenae and Amber, who were soft-spoken and more, um, girly.

"I can't hang out today," was my mantra for Marci, for about a month.

Then, on a chilly, February day just before Valentine's Day, my family moved from the neighborhood near Overland Elementary School to a new subdivision. We were the first inhabitants of a new house that Mom and Dad helped design.

It was a sprawling, ranch-style home on a quiet, leafy street named Rosewood.

Marci showed up on my doorstep a few days after we arrived. "I am sooo glad you're living here," she hummed. "I live right there!" she added, pointing to the backyard.

I shuddered. Mom, Dad, Annie and I had traded in our old house with cool Cheryl, who made Scotch-a-Roos with me, as our backyard neighbor... for *Marci!* I swallowed hard as Marci asked, yet again: "Do you want to come out and play? Maybe we could go to the rec center and play racquetball? You told me once that you played." Our new house was closer to the recreation center that my Grandpa West had built in 1986 when he was mayor. I loved going there to swim, ice skate and play racquetball. But to go there with Marci, who seemed to never stop talking?

"I can't come out," I replied. "I'm not allowed to have people over either, when my folks aren't here."

Marci arched an eyebrow. "Really? Why not?" she asked.

I had to think fast. I told her that I had to babysit my sister.

I knew Marci didn't quite believe me and I knew she would be back. And the following Saturday there she was, on my doorstep. "What about today?" she asked. "Do you have to babysit, or can you come out?" She then added, "I see your parents' car in the driveway so I know they're home."

Busted, I thought to myself. I looked around the living room, which was still piled high with boxes, the contents of which Mom had wanted me to start putting away. Anything was better than cleaning dusty glasses, I figured. "OK," I finally said, surprising Marci, whose eyes popped open in surprise. "I'll play a few games of racquetball with you."

By the end of the first set, I was hitting myself (literally, with the racquet, and also mentally) for taking nearly a month to agree to hang out with Marci. I had one of the best afternoons ever—of my entire life! All the thoughts and feelings about going to a new school melted away. It didn't matter that I was the new kid at school. It didn't matter that I was the new kid in the neighborhood. We played for two hours, laughing our way through our matches, as Marci raced around me to get a shot, and I threw myself on the court to reach some of mine. Occasionally, a stray ball ricocheted off my forehead. Several times, Marci and I were so overcome with laughter that we lay down on the surface of the court, tears streaming down our cheeks.

After our game, we went to her house for a pop and a piece of chocolate cake. In the family room in her basement, we talked—really talked. For the first time in my life, I had a real conversation with someone: about hopes and dreams for the future, about the other kids at school. Marci was also in transition, hoping to meet new people, because she had just moved to Rock Springs from another town. I could tell she was struggling with some of the same stuff I was. She didn't fit in anymore than I did. Yet we felt safe together.

"Marci," I said, when I zipped up my jacket to head home for dinner. "I am so glad you kept bugging me to hang out. I had an amazing time."

"Me too," Marci beamed. "I told you that you would like me!"

Marci and I became inseparable. We had weekend sleepovers at each other's houses—after some serious negotiations with our parents, who didn't approve, at first, of co-ed sleepovers. We hung out at school, before school, after school. About the only time we didn't hang out was when we were in the one or two classes we didn't take together. In Grade 8, we entered and won best Halloween costume—she dressed up as a carton of milk and I was a bag of groceries. I wore a plastic shopping bag as overalls and stuffed it with some of my sister's fake play food from her toy kitchen. We decorated my wheelchair to look like a shopping cart and painted my hair green with temporary spray paint and styled it to look like a head of lettuce.

Marci and I were more than best friends, really. During one sleepover, very early in the morning, Dad got up to go fishing. He heard something coming from the living room, where we were sprawled out in our sleeping bags. He walked in to find us both sound asleep, but talking to each other in our dreams. From that moment on, Mom and Dad always said our souls were talking to each other and that we had to be soulmates.

To this day, Marci still wears the silver bracelet that I gave her the Christmas before we both graduated high school. It's inscribed with the Celtic term: *Anam Cara.* One tradition says that after you marry your *anam cara,* or soul mate, you exchange the bracelet for a similar ring made out of gold. This is something that has always meant a lot to each of us. So much so that we now each have the term tattooed on our wrists. (Something to remind us of each other every day.)

Even when Marci moved away to Salt Lake City after our

sophomore year of high school, she continued to come back to Rock Springs to be my date at all the school dances, including junior and senior prom. She was even there watching from the audience as I walked across the stage to receive my high school diploma.

Another friend I made early in junior high was John. I had known him, a tall, skinny redheaded kid, since I took my first communion at Sts. Cyril and Methodius Church. We were the same age and usually in the same Sunday school class. John and I had never really liked one another and we had an unspoken rivalry. I was leery of his wild hand gestures, high energy and enthusiasm, and overwhelmed by how comfortable he was in his own skin. John later told me he was leery of me for *my* confidence. What we came to realize as young adults is that our rivalry came from our similarities: it was like we were both looking into a mirror. He was the Ron Weasley to my Harry Potter.

But back in Grade 7, when Marci invited me over to her house a few days after our first racquetball game and said John would be joining us, my gut reaction was to recite my mantra: "I can't hang out today." Yet I had learned enough from my experience with Marci to know that judging people without really getting to know them was hurting me, more than them.

"OK," I said to Marci. "I'll be right over."

At Marci's, John and I just sat on the couch drinking Sprite, while Marci tried to pry conversation from us. We eventually landed on the topic of music. That afternoon, I had been listening to Alanis Morissette's album *Jagged Little Pill*, and the song "All I Really Want." I broke out singing: "All I really want is some patience, a way to calm the angry voice."

To which John replied: "What I wouldn't give to find a soul mate. Someone else to catch this drift."

When he was done, John and I smiled and laughed. Thanks to Marci and Alanis, the ice had been broken. Our lifetime of friendship had begun.

We went on to spend the rest of the afternoon using Marci's Dad's camcorder to film the three of us in various scenes from television shows and the movies. In the middle of re-enacting a segment from William Shatner's *Rescue 911*—with John and I playing pregnant women in a car accident, and Marci trying desperately to save us—Annie showed up to bring me home for dinner.

I left knowing that from that day on, Marci, John and I would be a team—the three musketeers—inseparable and united, 'til death do us part!

I'd had a rocky start to junior high, but it soon became great, with Marci and John by my side. I felt I could take on anything. Well, anything, that is, until Patrick came into my life.

My middle school woes all began with my Dad and a simple statement: "Son, I think this would be good for you."

Dad and I were sitting on the couch in our living room. Strewn around him and on the coffee table were books on football, which he had Mom and me check out from the Sweetwater County Library. The television was set to mute. The Dallas Cowboys, Dad's favorite team and the team that would go on to claim the 1993 Super Bowl championship, was playing.

"OK," I said, swivelling around in my seat, trying to get as comfortable as I could for what I knew would be a very uncomfortable conversation.

"Son, football is about moving the ball down the field, sometimes by making small gains."

While Dad talked he showed me photographs from the books; pictures of big burly guys kicking footballs and tackling each other. Every now and then, Dad put a sticky note on a page he wanted me to read. "You don't need to know all the rules and plays, at least not to begin with," he said while flipping through a book that must have been an inch thick. "You're just the trainer. And that doesn't even mean you're really training anyone. You just need to make sure the guys on the team have their water bottles and equipment and if they're injured, well, I took a first aid course, so I can teach you how to wrap an ankle."

I rolled my eyes and my inner monologue said: *Dad takes one first aid course and thinks he is a paramedic. Typical Dad.*

"He doesn't need to know that," Mom shouted from the kitchen, where she was making turkey soup from scratch.

Dad wasn't listening. His eyes were glued to the television. "That was a terrible pass!" he shouted at Troy Aikman. He called Annie to come and join us. He sat her down in between him and me, slipped off one pink plastic princess slipper, and showed me how to wrap Annie's ankle, should she twist it playing football.

Dad, you see, had encouraged me to sign up to be the trainer for White Mountain's football team, the Panthers. My responsibilities involved attending all of the team's practices and games in the fall, and making sure the players were all there, in uniform and with their needs met. I knew *nothing* about football. I was the size of a kindergarten student. I didn't like the idea at first—not very much at all, to be honest. But Dad was overly excited. If I couldn't physically play on the team, he had found a way for me to be close to the sport, nonetheless. In the end, I came around to the idea, as it brought Dad and me closer together.

I was going to join the football team. Well, in a way.

For the first few weeks, I was absolutely petrified of my duties. For one, these guys were huge, even for middle school. Brock, for example, was well over six feet tall. I was perhaps two feet tall, when not in my wheelchair. Think of that visual for a second.

Also, junior high is when most kids are trying to find themselves, their styles and where they belong. Many of my friends from elementary school, like Amber and Jenae, now hung out with a different crew. John, Marci and I were certainly not sports stars—we were artsy and definitely on the fringe. We certainly weren't invited to the Friday night parties. But that was OK, and we did our own thing.

On one of our nights together, John and Marci shared some of their experiences of being bullied. Some of the kids at

White Mountain, as Marci put it, were "so desperate to show which clique they belonged to, that they put others down to try to prove they were cool." John admitted he had been called "gay" and "fag." He talked about being tripped in the hallway, slapped in the back of the head during class and called a girl. I had never experienced physical bullying like that but I had been called those names, too. Like everyone else, I just figured being bullied was a natural part of middle school. And after that conversation, I was really afraid that if anyone were to harass me, it would be the football players. After all, I was a logical target for the brunt of their jokes.

Initially, however, the boys on the team were very nice to me. They weren't giving me the high-fives they reserved for each other. Nor were they inviting me into their inner sanctum where they talked about the girls they had made out with. But they didn't bother me, either, like I feared they would. They just, well, accepted that I was there with what they needed. I was like Adam Sandler in *The Waterboy*.

But then things changed.

It was a rainy day in early spring. It seemed as if the hallways of White Mountain were more congested than usual. Kids in their muddied rain boots and slick raincoats and carrying pointy umbrellas were like an obstacle course for me as I made my way in my wheelchair from U.S. history to life science. The clouds outside the windows were so heavy that it seemed like nighttime, even though it was only about two in the afternoon. I had one class left for the day, then I was set to

Even at eight months I loved hanging out with my Mom and Dad.

I think this photo speaks for itself.

No photo from the 1980s would be complete without a fake background and stuffed bunny.

Dad, Annie and I. Just add water and our muscles turn into floaties.

This sums up my relationship with my Mom.

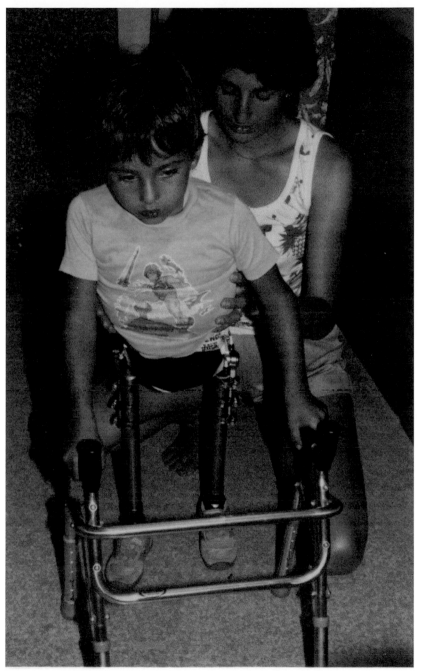

My first prosthetic legs. I know, I know, I look like a Transformer.

Annie and I. Is there any question that we aren't brother and sister?

John and I, soul mates. Here's a shot from the days when we had hair.

Reid West, my Dad's cousin, presenting me with my high school diploma.

The two most handsome men I know—me and my Dad after my university graduation.

Marci's wedding day. It's normal to ride on the bride's train, right?

Ms. Gigi Jasper and I in her classroom of English, mythology and activism.

Cheryl Ruffini and I reuniting after more than 10 years. She presented me with Scotch-a-Roos.

Grandma and Grandpa Callas and I. We're the original Jersey Shore *cast.*

Reed Cowan and I addressing the students of Emori Joi on my first trip to Kenya.

This is my activist pose or blue steel. You choose.

Me and the man himself, Jason Mraz. An unforgettable experience for me.

Ethan Zohn, from Survivor, and I having fun at We Day Vancouver 2010.

Me and some of my buddies from Sikirar in Kenya.

The kids in India were so helpful going down this hill, as they always are in India.

My Kenyan brother and Masaai guide Sankei and I. This photo sums up my love for Africa.

These schools aren't going to build themselves, people!

meet Marci and John. I had just shut my locker and was headed down the hall when I heard a voice from behind. I stopped and spun my wheelchair around. It was Patrick, a dark-haired and stocky football player.

"Spencer," he shouted again.

I was afraid that I would be late for class, so I kept going, just ignoring him. But Patrick quickly caught up to me. Then *bang!* First my books that were perched on the front of my wheelchair tumbled to the ground. And then I was on the cold floor, lying face down, one of my arms twisted underneath me. Patrick, whose mother had owned the daycare where my Mom worked when I was in kindergarten, had suddenly grabbed the back of my wheelchair. This caused it to stop suddenly, sending me plummeting to the floor.

Patrick stood off to the side, not moving. Both of us looked at each other, shocked, as students rushed by. Not knowing what to do, Patrick reached out to give me a hand up, but then pulled it away. He then ran down the hall. It all happened within the span of twenty seconds, but it felt like twenty minutes.

I groped around on the floor for my glasses. A bell sounded. I looked down. I could hear feet scurrying around me. My face was hot and my hands were perspiring from my embarrassment. I was choking back tears. Then the voices and the footsteps dimmed and eventually the hallway was empty.

I gathered up my books and pulled myself back into my wheelchair.

As Mr. Metz drew diagrams on the chalkboard on how to

dissect a squid, I found myself unable to concentrate. My head was tingling and I couldn't focus on anything. I just wanted to go home, go to my room, and get away. I could only stare at the raindrops landing on the window. I didn't even hear when Mr. Metz asked me a question.

"I... I..." I stuttered. "I'm sorry. I don't know." My classmates laughed as Mr. Metz pointed to someone else.

After school I didn't meet Marci and John, as planned. I headed straight to the handicapped bus that took me home on those few afternoons when I didn't have drama or football.

Judy, my bus driver, a dark-haired woman with a boisterous voice, beamed when she opened the door and saw me huddled by our designated pick-up spot. "Hey, Kiddo. No drama club today?" she asked. "Spencer..." she then said, more slowly. "Is something wrong?"

I shook my head. "No Judy," I replied. "I'm just not feeling that well."

"Get in here," she said, helping me onto the hydraulic device that lifted me and my wheelchair onto the bus.

I parked my wheelchair in my usual spot in the front and Judy went through her ritual of locking my chair to the floor. But unlike in the mornings when Judy and I would talk about everything from Wyoming's bad weather to the latest episode of *Seinfeld* to Britney Spears and Justin Timberlake, I was quiet.

I looked around at the other kids, all girls, who took the bus with me. One was hearing impaired. Another girl used an oxygen tank. Another girl had a mental or cognitive disability of sorts.

My head hung low. *I'm a misfit,* I thought to myself. Now,

I was upset about more than what had happened with Patrick. The event seemed to have ignited something deep down, something that I had never really dealt with before. At least not to the same extent, anyway. It was one of the first days in my life where I was reminded, in a negative way, that I was disabled or different.

I was bullied and the bully had preyed on my greatest vulnerability: my physical handicap.

For several days after, I would wake up in the morning and feel a crushing weight on my chest. I'd roll over, hit snooze on the alarm clock and go back to sleep, but then I'd force myself to get up when the alarm went off a second time. I didn't want anyone to know that I was dreading going to school. I didn't want anyone to know about what had happened.

But the pain weighed heavily on me. I picked at my food. I couldn't concentrate in class. I was gripped by fear that anyone and everyone I passed in the hallways at school could physically hurt me. I'd never felt like that before in my life, despite not having legs. I guess that's a sign of how lucky I was growing up.

When I finally had to share what happened to me with someone, I turned to Marci.

We were in child development class and we were working on a weeks-long assignment, for which we had to pretend flour sacks were our very own babies. I had to take my flour sack with me everywhere—school, the grocery store, home—and even put it to sleep at night. We had spent an entire class the week before coming up with names for our so-called babies. Marci had named her flour sack Jackson.

She wrapped Jackson in a baby blue blanket and listened patiently. When I was done telling her what happened with Patrick, she sighed. "Spence, I was in the girls' locker room before gym class a while ago. Several of the girls cornered me and started calling me all sorts of names like, 'dyke,' 'lesbo,' 'gay.'" All of the teasing had started because Marci happened to look over as one of the other girls was changing and it had made the girl uncomfortable.

"My face felt so red and hot. I wanted to scream at the girls in the locker room."

"When did it become OK to make someone feel so unwelcome?" I asked. "Why are our differences always singled out?"

"It sucks for us, Spence," Marci replied. "But be strong. My Mom says that by college, all of the 'it' people will be, well, either gone from our lives or more mature and nice."

"I guess so," I said, despite not feeling any better. Marci sat quietly for a second and then looked at me intently, calmly, and said, "Spence, why did you wait so long to tell me?" Embarrassed, I looked down at the floor. I didn't have an answer right away. I hadn't really thought of it—it was my issue and I was trying to deal with it.

"I thought if I told somebody, like you, my parents or even a teacher that I would be seen as a coward. Or that I couldn't fight my own battles." I then looked Marci straight in the eyes and said, "But I realize how crazy that sounds, and how much better I feel now that I told you. To get that off my chest and not hold it all in." The truth was bottling up inside of me. I didn't know where to turn at first. Talking with my closest friend took that all away, and didn't make me feel like a coward. It made me feel like I was standing up for myself.

After school that day I was back on the field for football practice. I played it cool, but inside I was shaking when Patrick came out onto the turf. He didn't even look at me, though. He just ignored me and went on like nothing had happened. In fact, I had very little contact with him at all after that. Which was good, I suppose, although I wish I'd been able to learn why he did what he did. Sometimes, though, I guess there's not always a reason.

In Grade 10, I heard that he was killed in a tragic car accident. I had mixed emotions when I learned of his death at first. I was very sad for his family, but part of me was still angry for allowing him to make me feel less than human. I was also angry at myself for not finding a way to tell him how he made me feel. To let him know what kind of an impact his actions had on me.

There were a few other bullying incidents in junior high. A boy in Grade 7 was so curious as to how I went to the washroom, that one day, in the locker room before gym class, he stormed right up in front of me, stood so close I could feel his hot breath on my cheek, and said: "I don't believe you are like every other guy below the waist. I am going to kick you in the nuts to find out."

He didn't, but, let me tell you, it was a confrontation that really upset me.

(Even to this day, someone inevitably asks after my speeches: "How do you go to the washroom?" I understand the curiosity, but let me say this once and for all: All my parts are intact and I do everything everyone else does just fine, thank you very much.)

By the end of Grade 9, the end of junior high, I was finding my way. I was confident and secure in the person I was becoming. So much so that when the head of the theater program at high school, Mr. Keller, opened auditions for *Seven Brides for Seven Brothers* to students in junior high, I decided to try out. A girl named Megan and I had been taking choir classes all through middle school and we were told we were very strong singers.

"Are you nervous?" Megan asked. "I hear Mr. Keller needs tenors. And you, Spence, can definitely hold your own."

Meagan and I both landed parts in the chorus of the high school musical and our final semester of middle school was spent racing back and forth for practices in the big auditorium of the school I would start attending in Grade 10.

When I wasn't rehearsing for the play, I was at White Mountain Junior High or working. I had two jobs, both unpaid. The first was as an office aid. I received a credit for taking that wheelchair of mine, which I had decorated with bumper stickers (one said *Feel Free to Point, Stare, Whisper and Ask Questions*), all around the school, picking up the attendance records. I would then plop myself down on the counter in the office and file the papers while listening to Joanne and the other office staff gossip about faculty members, students and the administration.

My second job was as the computer science teacher's assistant. Mr. Biedschied was one of those teachers that every student loves. He was easygoing, funny and really focused on helping us develop a love of computers. He got so excited back then when someone began to navigate the Internet for the first time. It was 1994, after all, and the Internet was new—not just for us, but most of the world. Mr. Biedschied also had this great personality tick. When he was flustered we all knew it, because he would talk non-stop but not get anywhere, like: "Ok... so... then, anyway..." We would all just stare at him and smile.

My job was to help Mr. Biedschied hook up wires, fix the machines and order equipment. Just as with my office duties, I got a school credit for doing so. Mr. Biedschied liked to call me Sister Mary Spencer, after Molly Shannon's character, Mary Katherine Gallagher, on *Saturday Night Live*. When he did, I would slip my hands under my armpits, just like Mary Katherine would do on the TV show.

It came as a big surprise to me, when, at my junior high graduation, I won Business Student of the Year for my work with Mr. Biedschied and, to a lesser extent, for volunteering in the office. I wheeled myself proudly out on stage and collected my plaque.

There was a moment at the graduation prom when Marci and I fell silent. The lyrics to the song I had sung as part of the chorus in *Seven Brides for Seven Brothers* drifted to my mind:

Born to laugh, born to dream.

Born to spread your light.

In the past few years, I'd had lots of light around me: John, Marci, my teachers and my family. And boy, I loved to dream. (I still love to dream.) My dreams that summer would be all about high school, honing my acting skills and taking the lead in a school play the following year.

Chapter 6

Since I had ended junior high performing in the big leagues—the high school musical—I thought that the next logical step was for me to become the "star." My minor role in *Seven Brides for Seven Brothers* would be my pass to a better, perhaps leading role in the next production, I thought. So, when I started high school, I waited with bated breath for Mr. Keller's announcement of what the fall musical would be and when he was holding auditions. What I loved about performing in theater is that for an hour or so I got to create a character, and, for an evening, completely live in that character's world.

When I couldn't take the wait any longer, I asked Mr. Keller what musical he had chosen. He told me that the fall play would be *West Side Story*, and then handed me the script. As soon as I got home I began rehearsing the song "Maria" that the character Tony, who I was auditioning to play, sang. A few weeks later, I walked on my hands out to center stage and thought my audition was flawless. I was confident I nailed the role.

But a week later, my heart sank. When Mr. Keller posted the names for the show, my eyes scanned up and down the list. Finally I found my name at the bottom, beside the heading *Assistant Director*. I was speechless. If I wasn't Tony, I thought I would at least be in the ensemble. That I wouldn't even be on stage was something that had not crossed my mind. Mr. Keller explained to me during our next meeting that the assistant director was very important. I would help the cast with their lines, make sure everyone was on the stage where they were supposed to be and, during the actual performance, work backstage following the script and calling the cues.

"Spencer," Mr. Keller concluded. "There is a lot of dancing in *West Side Story*. I thought it would be best if you were the assistant director instead." I really appreciated Mr. Keller making an effort to include me but I nonetheless interpreted his words as: "Because you are in a wheelchair, you can't dance."

Like everything in life, I embraced my role as assistant director and had fun with it. The other kids in the production enjoyed my direction so much that, in the spring, the cast members rewarded my hard work by giving me a part in the student production of *Broadway Dreams*. I sang some of the solo lines in "I Hope I Get It!" from the musical *A Chorus Line*.

As a result, I entered Grade 11 with my theater ego intact. I was going for the lead again, this time in the winter production of *The Music Man*. I spent every evening and spare weekend moment practising the song "Seventy-six Trombones." Once again, I didn't get the lead, and I was, at first, disappointed. But Mr. Keller did give me the part of one of the school board members, which involved singing in a barbershop quartet. Me and three other guys rehearsed night and day to make sure our harmony was dead on for the songs "Lida Rose" and "It's You." In fact, both Mr. Keller and our choir teacher, Mr. Starks, who was helping us with the music, said we were going to steal the show. Part of my costume on stage was a blanket over my lap, so the audience would think I had legs. Of course, being from a small town most people knew the truth, but hey, it was acting!

As predicted, our performance did steal the show. We received a standing ovation from the audience. Mr. Keller said the Barbershop Quartet outdid themselves and then he personally congratulated us for our hard work. *Finally*, I thought. *I've broken through*. For sure I would get a leading role in the next play, *Oklahoma*.

Sadly, it was a repeat of *West Side Story*. I didn't get a part and it was very difficult for me to not take it personally. "Mr. Keller knows what I can do," I said to myself before bed one night. "I have proven myself, proven I can sing and act! It has to be because I'm in a wheelchair. There can be no other reason."

Whatever the real reason, on the final night of the performance, a balmy Wyoming evening, Mr. Keller approached me. "Spence," he began. "Next year, we're doing a play with a part that I think may be right up your alley."

And, indeed, in the fall of 1998, during my Grade 12 year at Rock Springs High School, I finally had a leading role. I played the nerd in the musical *The Yearbook*. My character, Conrad, was bullied and picked on for being different and intelligent. Conrad wasn't good in sports—he got straight A's and he wasn't very popular.

The autumn of 1998 was a fitting time for me to play Conrad. For October 12 of that year was one of the darkest days in Wyoming's history, and certainly the darkest day for all of us young people who were different, like me, John and Marci.

With overt bullying nonexistent, now just a part of my middle school memories, I had settled into just being me. (OK, the implicit bullying, like exclusion from one group or another, was still going on; as was the name-calling, but John, Marci and I didn't care. We had each other. We knew who we were and refused to let anyone else tell us otherwise.) And by this time I also had a vehicle, so Marci, John and I could take mini-adventures around the city. Grandpa West had bought me a blue minivan, and Grandpa and Grandma Callas had bought me a gold licence plate that had my name on it. I had my driver's licence in my wallet and a special hand control that allowed me to brake and push the speed pedals, while steering at the same time. On the day that I received my license, my Mom gave me a silver cross on a keychain that read: "Spence, you need all the help you can get."

Just to digress, I nearly didn't get my driver's licence, by the way. On my sixteenth birthday, when I stood in line at the counter to fill out the paperwork, the receptionist asked: "Height?" I replied: "Two feet, seven inches." The computer beeped and she apologized. "I am sorry," she said. "The computer won't accept a height of less than three feet for a driver. Do you mind if I embellish your answer?" I nodded, and to this day, my driver's licence says I am three feet tall.

But on October 12, 1998, Marci, John and I became all too aware that while we thought our differences were accepted and that we were cool in our own skin, that might not be the case.

Matthew Shepard was a twenty-one-year-old political science student at the University of Wyoming in Laramie, which was about four hours from Rock Springs. He was gay. On October 6, 1998, two young men picked Matthew up at a bar and then took him to a desolate location overlooking the twinkling lights of Laramie's downtown core. They pistol-whipped him, beat in his head and then tied him to a split-pole fence. He was found the next day, so badly beaten that the person who discovered him thought he was a scarecrow, until he saw Matthew's dirty blonde hair, blowing in the breeze. Matthew was barely conscious and died on October 12 from his head wounds.

At the time, John and I were at a state-wide church retreat in Cheyenne, Wyoming, about forty-five minutes from Laramie. We were representing none other than Sts. Cyril and Methodius Catholic Church. When we first learned about Matthew Shepard, all we knew was that a boy had been beaten up pretty bad. We started a collection to help his family pay for his hospital bills.

But when the media, in the hundreds, descended on the

sleepy town of Laramie, and it came out that Matthew was attacked because he was gay, we all felt gut-wrenched, like it could have been one of us. Anyone that was *different*.

There were protests and marches in many of America's major cities. There were calls from coast to coast, from the likes of President Bill Clinton, Madonna and Ellen Degeneres, for new legislation addressing hate crimes. But Wyoming is a right wing, predominantly Christian conservative state. With less than a million people, Wyoming has the lowest population of any state in America. Despite our rich immigrant history, modern-day Wyoming is seen by most of the rest of America as Cowboy Country. For some, including Marci, John and me, the goal was to get out: not only from Rock Springs, but Wyoming, period.

Matthew Shepard had done so, traveling with his family to places like Morocco, but he returned to Wyoming because he appreciated the state as well, as Matthew's Dad summed up in a letter he eventually read at his son's murderer's trial. "When Matthew was left to die in the field, tied to the fence," his father said, "he was not alone. There were his life-long friends with him. First he had the beautiful night sky and the same stars and moon we saw through the telescope. Then he had the daylight and the sun to shine on him. And through it all, he was breathing in the scent of the pine trees, from the snowy range. He heard the wind, the ever-present Wyoming wind, for the last time."

People who were close to Matthew said he was compassionate and caring, likely on his way to doing humanitarian work of some kind as a career. Some people who didn't know Mathew said he got what was coming to him because he was gay. The independent Baptist minister Fred Phelps even came to Wyoming with a posse in tow—waving placards that said homosexuality was a sin—and protested at Matthew's funeral.

John, in particular, was hit hard. Matthew's murder pulled him inside himself. He became, for a while, shy, aloof and introspective—and for good reason. A year later, he himself would be admitting to people, including me, that he was gay.

But I've gotten ahead of myself.

Back in 1998, our final year of high school, we all had to come to terms with the hate in our state. Then, not long after that, in the early spring of 1999, Rock Springs High School was rocked by a series of bomb threats. Every six weeks or so, the fire alarm would go off and we would shuffle our way outside. During one of the bomb scares there must have been about a thousand people standing on the football field, in the snow, prompting one student to say: "We're like cattle here. If someone really is aiming to get us, they have us all here, in one place."

We had one of these bomb scares on another haunting day of my final year of high school—the day of the Columbine shootings.

Columbine is a suburb of Denver, and about a seven-hour drive away from us. On April 20th, 1999, just two months before my high school graduation, Eric Harris and Dylan Klebold walked into Columbine High School, shot and killed twelve students and a teacher, and injured another twenty-four. News reports went on at length about how Dylan and

Eric were "different." They were the outsiders. They were my age. They were in their last year of high school, like me, and they retaliated. "You know, Spence, I heard Columbine happened because those guys were bullied," John said one day, wild-eyed. "As dark as this may sound, and you know I would never in a million years hurt anyone, not even a fly, as much as we've been made fun of and harassed, I can almost understand where they came from. This could easily have happened in our school."

My innocent world of Sunday family dinners, trying to get the best parts in the school plays and making movies with Marci and John was collapsing around me. I felt a constant unease everywhere I went, especially if I was alone at night. To make matters worse, John and I were taking a class with Ms. Jasper at the far end of the school on the second floor. The room had two small windows that never opened. "Spence," John whispered to me another time. "After everything that has happened lately, I get nervous coming to Ms. Jasper's class. Think about it. We are on the second floor, with nowhere to go. I can't help but imagine all of us huddled in a corner. We'd be trapped like rats!"

"Whoa, relax," I half laughed, half groaned. "You're gonna give yourself shingles if your stress levels get any higher." But the truth was, I was very afraid, too. I thought of my Mom, Dad and sister. I thought of my whole family. I trembled, for my worst fear was to be without them. *What if something does happen to me?* I asked myself, many times. It was a scary, unnerving thought.

The answer, of course, was right in front of me—for answers usually are. I just didn't know it at the time. You see, in that same classroom, where John felt so boxed in, also stood our teacher, Ms. Gigi Jasper, a short, feisty, African-American woman with stylish black high-heeled shoes, red lipstick, wild, curly hair and a kick-ass way of teaching. In Grade 10, John and I had her for English. While we read the assigned books, like *To Kill a Mockingbird,* our class discussions always wound their way through modern-day politics, social issues, religion, race relations—you name it, we talked about it. Ms. Jasper's assignments were really creative, too. Once I had to write a paper using only one-syllable words. My topic was my height and how I went through an entire day constantly being reminded that I was short, only to arrive home for dinner and be given *shrimp* to eat.

Ms. Jasper taught Grade 12 mythology in much the same way as she taught Grade 10 English. "OK, class," she said one day, in her high-pitched, almost childlike voice. "This has been a challenging year for all of you—Matthew Shepard's murder, the bomb scares, Columbine. But I don't think there is much difference between people now and three thousand years ago. We wrestle with the same problems. New incarnations perhaps, such as kids killing kids because they're popular, or kids killing kids because they're different. But it's the same problems retold or relived in different ways, like an ancient myth. So what do we do? How do we make sense of this?"

In a way, her mythology class was where my own personal journey began—or at least the inward one.

Looking back, mythology was the best class that I took in all of my years at school, including university. We students were arranged in a semicircle facing Ms. Jasper's desk, which was littered with magazines from *Vanity Fair* to *Mother Jones*, and books by everyone from Karl Marx to Toni Morrison. Sometimes my eyes would scan the classroom, which Ms. Jasper had decorated wall to wall with posters of people including playwright Lorraine Hansberry, author Amy Tan, birth control advocate Margaret Sanger and baseball player Babe Ruth. But more often than not, I would perch my torso up on the back of my chair and remain glued to Ms. Jasper's every word.

"So all of these gods and goddesses, mortal heroes and semi-mortal heroes that we've been reading about," Ms Jasper said, in a class near the end of term, "set out on a journey. One of my favorite writers, Joseph Campbell, calls it the 'hero's journey.' It is more or less the same for everyone, even all of us, although the obstacles we face and the personal growth we achieve on our own hero's journey are unique. So, first question," she continued, tapping her fingernails on her desk. "Often the hero starts out where?"

Silence filled the room. Ms. Jasper rolled her eyes. "Come on you Sweet Baboos," she exclaimed. Ms. Jasper liked to call her students the same name Sally, from *Peanuts*, called Linus. "This should be fun, for the hero's journey is yours, too."

"Let's take *The Odyssey*," Ms. Jasper pressed on. "You all remember that, right?" Ms. Jasper knew that probably only a handful of us, including me, were paying attention when we read the classic tale during class. But she feigned ignorance. "It took the Greek hero King Odysseus ten years to get home to Ithaca after the Trojan War. Why? Because after the war, Poseidon captures him. Meanwhile, back home, Odysseus's wife, Penelope, is fending off suitors. Odysseus's son, Telemachus, is harboring all sorts of conflicting emotions about his Dad. He's angry, but also striving to become a man worthy of his father's legend. Odysseus is offered immortality by the sea goddess Calypso if he agrees to be her husband. She tells him that his wife will have aged, but she, Calypso, will remain eternally young. Odysseus wants Penelope and turns down the offer."

"What a fool," a burly football player in the back mumbled. "Give me a young goddess any day!"

Ignoring the laughter that filled the room, Ms. Jasper asked: "Where does Odysseus's journey begin?"

"When he's captured," John piped up.

"And then what happens?" Ms. Jasper probed.

"He's tested," another girl in class remarked. "In fact, everyone around Odysseus is tested—his wife, his son and him."

"I think Odysseus's journey started long before his meeting with Calypso," John jumped in. "I think Odysseus, although strong, needed to go away from the people he loved most, to realize how important they were to him."

"Interesting, John," Ms. Jasper replied, putting her hands on her hips.

"I think of the tarot cards when I think of the hero's journey," a girl interjected. "We all start out the fool and go on our missions. In Odysseus's case, his mission was to go home, for isn't that what we all want in the end? To go home—to our real homes, the ones we know are in our hearts. It's getting there that is the battle—sometimes a lifelong battle."

At that, the bell sounded and we could, indeed, all go home.

"I want all of you to come to the next class prepared to tell me about some of the gods or goddesses you like and can relate to," Ms. Jasper called out, as we bundled up our bags.

I thought about all of the gods and goddesses I'd been learning about in class as I drove home. Just as I hit the main street, the CD in my stereo changed to the soundtrack from Disney's *Hercules*. "Hercules!" I said out loud. "I think I like Hercules the most."

Hercules is the Roman name for the Greek god Heracles. Hercules had a god for a father, the ever-mighty Zeus, and a mortal for his mother, Alcmene. Zeus's wife, Hera, obviously didn't like having little Hercules around, the son from one of her husband's affairs, so when the boy was young she sent two spitting, poisonous snakes to kill him. Tiny, yet super-strong Hercules just strangled them.

As I learned in Ms. Jasper's class, all heroes have a downfall—or Achilles' heel. In Hercules's case, Hera drove him mad, so much so that he killed his own children.

Eurystheus, the king of Tiryns and Mycenae and a cousin of Hercules, ordered Hercules to perform twelve impossible tasks as punishment for his crime. Hercules was first ordered to slay the Nemean lion, whose skin could not be penetrated by spears or arrows. Hercules, who possessed impossible strength, killed it with his bare hands. The twelfth task in-

volved Hercules bringing Cerberus from Hades (the under-
world, or kingdom of the dead). Luckily, Hercules was wearing
the Nemean lion's skin, which made him immune to Cerberus,
who had razor sharp teeth and a venomous snake for a tail.

"I love Hercules's strength and endurance," I told Ms. Jasper during our next mythology class. "He boldly faced every
challenge presented to him and triumphed."

"Many of you may not realize this yet," Ms. Jasper said,
addressing everyone. "But we are all tested in life, again and
again and again. And if we are wise, if we are courageous, if
we see the positive, even in the middle of the negative, we will
learn something from our previous tests that will help us in
overcoming our present dilemmas."

I thought of Hercules wearing the lion's skin, then I thought
of myself, back at the start of middle school, when Amber and
Jenae moved on to new friends. Magically, John and Marci
appeared. John and Marci, both different like me, helped me
stay strong in the face of my bullies. They also kept me optimistic when I never got the roles I tried out for in theater.
"Spence, Wyoming is the small-time stage. Just wait until the
world sees you," Marci would say. John would add his own
twist: "All good performers go through the muck. Look at Madonna. She had to climb her way to the top and now she is one
of the greatest! Remember, you have to go through *it* to get *it*!"
"Spencer," Ms. Jasper said, when the bell rang at the end of
class one day. "Can you hang around for a bit?"

I watched as a girl and a boy played with Ms. Jasper's light
switch, a small painting of Michelangelo's *David*, on their way

out. The statue's genitalia was cut out and the light switch was in its place. "Tick, tick, tick," the girl said, turning the light on and off, while the boy laughed.

"Spencer!" Ms. Jasper called out. "Having fun?"

I nearly jumped out of my chair, blushing from having been caught watching the boy and girl flirting with each other. I wheeled up beside Ms. Jasper's desk.

"You know, Spencer," Ms. Jasper said, looking at me with her dark brown eyes. "Do you think you are living a hero's myth?"

I started to laugh. "I don't think so. I'm just plain old me. Not sure how I would be a hero."

"Oh, so you think," she replied, in a slow, deep voice, which I knew meant she was serious. "We're always living the hero's journey. Sometimes the challenges are harder than in other times. Life is like an ocean, after all, there are high tides and low tides."

"Yes," I replied, thinking of Ms. Jasper, whom I had heard was going through her own never-ending low tide. In 1994, a white student threw a desk at Ms. Jasper and then swore at her. Now, Ms. Jasper is a peace-loving teacher who listens to Billy Holiday and Etta James and recites quotes from inspirational leaders, like Gandhi: "First they ignore you. Then they laugh at you. Then they fight you. Then you win!" She only wanted the school to get the boy to apologize. The principal wanted him expelled and scheduled a hearing with the school board to review the case. The boy showed up at the hearing with a lawyer, and that's when Ms. Jasper's nightmares began. The school board no longer wanted to talk to Ms. Jasper.

Ms. Jasper wasn't exactly sure why no one would return her phone calls or talk to her about the case. The boy was still at school, so Ms. Jasper, fearing for her own physical safety, got her sister, a lawyer, involved. Ms. Jasper was searching for answers. *Where is my apology? What happened in that school board meeting when the lawyer showed up? Am I safe?* Ms. Jasper was demanding equality, for surely, in those days in Wyoming, if a black student had thrown a desk at a white teacher, the student would have been out of the school for good.

When Ms. Jasper's sister took on the case, Ms. Jasper's home, a bungalow she shared with her husband, was vandalized. Kids tossed eggs against her brick walls more times than she can remember. And worse, someone even shot bullets at her front window in an attempt to get her and her sister to back down. Finally, in the fall of 1997, the boy wrote his apology letter and sold his truck to compensate Ms. Jasper for her time and stress. She also sued the school district—and won— for putting her in an unsafe work environment.

Ms. Jasper is not one to ride the low tides hanging onto a life rope, just praying she survives. She decided in the middle of all of this to get her Ph.D. in education, taking courses during the summer months and writing her papers in her off-hours from teaching. She said to me once that she had to pick a school that most of her students would never get into. "I knew I had to make myself bulletproof, unlike my house, so that no student or principal or school board would take me for granted again. I had to go to a school that was at the top of the heap." Ms. Jasper went to New York University and spent three summers at Trinity College at Oxford University in England. Her Ph.D. dissertation, not surprisingly, profiled the stories of—and examined the quite rare phenomenon of—black American educators teaching all-white classes. Ms. Jasper documented three such situations: all three teachers, four including her, were teachers in states she called "lily white, like Wyoming."

One of Ms. Jasper's dissertation subjects, a male teacher in Iowa, had white students carving hangman nooses into their wooden desks. He received anonymous hate letters on a regular basis. "You know what this teacher's principal did, Spencer?" Ms. Jasper said to me. "The principal told this black teacher, 'Boys will be boys!' So this poor man quit teaching. Who knows, maybe I would have quit, if I didn't have my husband standing beside me, and my lawyer sister."

When everyone had left the classroom, including the boy and girl playing with the light switch, Ms. Jasper asked me: "I've been wondering why you identify most with Hercules. I am curious as to why you picked someone with supernatural strength."

"He's interesting," I replied. "He's half god, half mortal. I like his internal struggle of finding out who he is with this superhuman strength, but not understanding where it comes from. I like that he is always faced with these huge challenges, but overcomes them."

"Yes," Ms. Jasper said, nodding. "The first time I met you, Spencer, I was visiting Overland Elementary School as a substitute teacher. You were eight-years-old. You were in your wheelchair and you came up to me and said: 'Want to see something that drives my teachers crazy?' You then flung yourself out of your wheelchair and landed on the floor. I have always been fascinated by your confidence. That I could be suckered by an eight-year-old. I have always known you were going to make it in life, no matter what obstacles were put in your path. Inside of you are a Batman *and* a Superman. Your challenge is whether you will allow your shell," she said, pointing to my wheelchair, "to hold you back."

"Spencer," Ms. Jasper added, "you have also always reminded me of the Greek god Hephaestus. He is referred to as the ugly one because his legs are all messed up."

"Oh," I said lowering my head and thinking, *Well, I much preferred thinking of myself as Superman.*

"There are different theories as to how Hephaestus's legs get messed up," Ms. Jasper continued, ignoring my blushing cheeks. "One story is that his mother, Hera, and her husband, Zeus, were fighting because Zeus was fooling around with a mortal woman. Hephaestus got in the middle and Zeus was so angry he threw Hephaestus out of Olympus, and he bashed his legs up in the process. However, Hephaestus came to be a very cool guy. He invented robots that could walk for him. He could make anything, for that matter. He was resourceful. That is you, Spencer. Look at yourself! You don't have super-human strength," she said, "but you have your wits, you have internal strength, you have your heart and you find ways to make things work with what you have."

"Do you really think so?" I asked. "I just … I'm just not so sure anymore. All of the stuff that has happened this year has been really confusing to me. Why do people *hate* so much? I can't help but wonder what's around the corner for me. Is there someone out there who hates *me* so much that they'll attack me when I least suspect it? The way the kids at Columbine were attacked; the way Matthew Shepard was targeted?"

"Just live your own journey, Spencer. Be on guard, but live your own life, and I hope you will never have to face discrimination the way Matthew Shepard did. We have all been placed on earth with the potential to be superheroes, to do something great, to rise above our challenges and set an example for others. This world so needs examples of greatness right now. Don't cower because you feel unworthy, or self-conscious about being different. Be great. Show others what greatness can be, so they can find it inside of them, too."

Many years later, I recalled that life-changing talk I had with Ms. Jasper after reading a quote from well-known American author Marianne Williamson. As she put it:

Our deepest fear is not that we are inadequate. Our deepest fear is that we are powerful beyond measure. It is our light, not our darkness that most frightens us. We ask ourselves, Who am I to be brilliant, gorgeous, talented, fabulous? Actually, who are you not to be? Your playing small does not serve the world ... We are all meant to shine, as children do ... And as we let our own light shine, we unconsciously give other people permission to do the same.

Chapter 7

In the past few years, I've had the opportunity to meet many great people worldwide—from Kenya to China, from India to Canada. And I've heard and read about how some of the great people in this world knew, starting when they were small children, that they were meant to do something important in this world—to live *big*, or as Williamson says, *shine*. The stories of Mother Teresa and Elie Wiesel, for example, have inspired me. And Matthew Shepard's father was all too aware that children, all children, are destined for something. For in that same talk he gave at the trial, he also said: "My son Matthew did not look like a winner. He was uncoordinated and wore braces from the age of thirteen to the day he died. Although, in his all-too-brief life he proved he was a winner. I keep wondering the same thing I did when I first saw him in the hospital ... what would he have become?

How could he have changed his piece of the world, to make it better?"

As for me, I didn't have any such *knowing,* and I'm not so sure those around me did, either. I knew I was going to live a long life, and I was not aware that the doctors and nurses were afraid that I would die during my high school years. I was also unaware that they had expressed these fears to my Mom and Dad. Mom was very good at protecting me from her worries, doubts and fears. But I never felt I was special. In fact, I spent the first part of my life just trying to fit in. I never felt a *calling.* I never felt something stir inside of me. That is, until just before my high school graduation in 1999.

I was on the cheerleading squad. Oh yes. I was a Rock Springs High School cheerleader. I didn't wave pom-poms, but I wore a cool black shirt, which matched the girls' dresses, with the word *TIGERS* written on the front in orange and white lettering. I was one of three boys in my graduating year to be on the first ever co-ed Rock Springs cheerleading squad. I cheered for the football team in the fall and the basketball team in the spring. And if ever there was a moment during that tumultuous Grade 12 year when I did feel afraid, really afraid—like the bull's-eye on a target—it was in March, when my squad headed to the cheerleading state championships in Casper, Wyoming.

The event center in Casper was jam-packed with parents, friends and basketball players from all the high schools around the state. The cheerleading competition was being held right before the basketball state championships. Even the media were out, wanting something positive to report on.

Throughout most of the other cheerleading performances, the jocks on the basketball teams were screaming, howling, whistling and jeering no matter how much athleticism the cheerleaders put into their routines, including the throws and tumbling. Really, the athletes never considered what we did a sport. Aunt Jamie, sitting in the stands right underneath one of these teams, said to me afterward: "When you came out on the gymnasium floor, I thought, *Oh no, what are they going to say now?*" She had good reason to worry. Back in Rock Springs, during some of the football and basketball games, players used to laugh at us boy cheerleaders, pointing their fingers and whispering things like "What are they, girls?" and "gay" and "fags" under their breath.

But when our squad came out at the state championships, the audience turned quiet.

Our music—"C'mon 'n Ride It (The Train)" and Survivor's "Eye of the Tiger"—came on and we automatically went into action. We all paraded out, doing our jumps, somersaults and cartwheels. The two other boys on the squad lifted the girls high on their shoulders, with Herculean strength. We were all pumped, moving on adrenalin we'd never experienced before. Then the spotlight turned on me for my solo move: a handstand, right into a somersault and then the splits (with my arms, of course). I held my breath and performed it perfectly. It felt like the music was whizzing by, yet it seemed to last forever at the same time.

And that is when it happened.

During one of my lifts, when I was about six feet in the air, I felt a certain *stirring* for the very first time. I felt a part of something—part of a team that was about to achieve something great, part of a team that was about to do something groundbreaking. It was a feeling that I was where I was meant to be exactly at that moment. And it was a feeling that I was being called to do something.

After the performance, the audience, including the jocks, gave our squad a standing ovation. Jamie's son, my cousin Mitchell, was in the audience, too. He was just a small child then, but when he grew up to become a football star, he summed it up best when he said: "We athletes know when someone deserves respect. And what you did out there was awesome!"

Our squad took home the state cheerleading championship, which the school had ordered us to do. One of the reasons Debbie, our coach, had made the team co-ed was that she wanted cheerleading to be recognized by the high school as a bona fide sport and qualify for funding for uniforms and travel. "Sure," the principal had said. "Just bring me home a state championship and you can have your status and your money." To do this, Debbie knew she had to be over the top. She knew she had to mix it up a bit.

I was proud to be on the team that year and the legacy I helped leave Rock Springs with—its first cheerleading championship. But mostly I was proud because for the first time I felt my true potential.

My cheerleading days all started in the spring of 1998, the

final months of my Grade 11 year. I was seventeen. I wore my Rock Springs High School black and orange letterman jacket with two letters sewn on the back—one for choir, which I was still doing, and the other for drama. I felt, however, like John Travolta at the end of the movie, *Grease*—I was missing something. I was missing a letter for athletics.

There is this tacit rule that in order to be considered well-rounded students, you need to be good at both academics and sports. Mom had put me in gymnastics lessons when I was a small child and I had thought in middle school that I would try out for the Rock Springs High School gymnastics team. But in Grade 10, just as I started high school, the boys' gymnastics team was cancelled because there weren't enough boys interested. And realistically, there was no other sport that I could do. Yet, it was a jagged pill for me to swallow, particularly in Grade 11. You see, that year my Grandpa West took Dad and me to South Africa's Kalahari Desert to hunt gemsboks and wildebeests. Grandpa West, by this time, was semi-retired. He was a member of Safari Club International and spent part of his leisure time traveling to the great hunting locations of the world. His homes in Rock Springs and Arizona—and even his cabin—are adorned with trophies from his kills, including a stuffed lion, a stuffed caribou, a bearskin rug and antlers. They cover the walls just about everywhere.

Since I was a young child, I had often gone hunting with Dad and Grandpa West. When I was really little, Dad would put me in a backpack and carry me through the wilds of Wyoming. When I was old enough to hold a gun, I would drive the four-wheeler and hunt antelope alongside Dad. But I never liked hunting. To this day, I believe I should not have the power to take another life. And that trip to South Africa highlighted for me the differences between the West men and myself. I was much more like my mother, who liked to read, cook, shop, do arts and crafts, listen to music and have long conversations over very large dinners. My Dad and Grandpa were the outdoorsmen.

But while I came to the realization that I was not a *sportsman*, I still wanted something to fill that void, something to show I was an athlete, but in my own way. So when Debbie, the coach of the cheerleading squad, posted the notice that she was opening the team up to males, I decided right away to try out. A part of me knew that the admissions officers at colleges liked applications which showed the students excelling in sports. And another part of me was thinking that since I would never be a hunter, maybe Dad and Grandpa West would be proud of cheerleading instead.

What I didn't know was that Debbie wasn't so sure she wanted me on the team. "Spencer could get hurt," she told my Mom. "We have people way up in the air. Someone could fall on him."

"Debbie," Mom said, gently, like she did starting way back with Grandma Callas. "Spencer is going to do what he wants to do. He knows how to look after himself. He just wants to be like everyone else."

Truth be told, there were only four boys brave enough in the entire school to try out—one of them ended up quitting and the other one was Debbie's own son, Carl. We all got together every day for a week leading up to the big audition day and practised basic cheers and simple tumbling. The night before the auditions, right after a dinner of pork chops, gravy and rice, Mom said to me: "Spencer, I'm really proud of you for trying out for cheerleading. But I want you to be realistic. You might not get a spot on the team. Cheerleading is harder than most people think."

My eyes turned downcast.

"Spencer, I've just seen you get your hopes up and then have them come crashing down with the high school musicals," Mom continued. "It's OK if you are not on a sports team. You make me so proud, just being you."

Mom ruffled my short-cropped black hair and I started to laugh. The two of us then rehearsed one of my cheers, a cheer she also did when she was a Rock Springs High School cheerleader.

We ain't bad because we know we're good.

We're going to walk on the wolves, like we walk on wood.

Hey… Hey… Hey… Hey…

Be Aggressive. Be Aggressive. Be A-G-G-R-E-S-S-I-V-E!

Of course, I made the team. I spent that summer practising routines with the entire squad. We also washed cars and decorated some of the shop windows in downtown Rock Springs to pay for our uniforms, and even made an athletic calendar, posting the dates and times of all of the upcoming sporting events.

On top of cheerleading, I was also working for Rock Springs' Chamber of Commerce raising money for college. My official job was as an information specialist, a.k.a. a receptionist. My job was to hand out pamphlets on interesting places for tourists to go and give visitors directions to motels, hotels and restaurants. A lot of tourists from Asia and the east coast of the United States traipsed by my desk, en route to what my state was best known for: Grand Teton National Park in northwestern Wyoming and Yellowstone National Park, which is spread across northwestern Wyoming, Montana and Idaho. "There's even a Grand Canyon of the Yellowstone there, which has two waterfalls, right on top of each other," I would tell the visitors.

I could sense, at first, that many of the tourists were a little surprised when I leapt up on the counter. But the look of shock in their eyes soon disappeared as I calmly and professionally offered them directions to Wyoming hot spots or explained our history. "Rock Springs imprisoned Butch Cassidy, and local lore says that when he got out of jail he hid a vast treasure in the mountains out there," I would say, pointing to the hills that could be seen from the large bay window. "And that treasure, well, it has never been found."

"Really," the tourists would gasp, no longer wondering why I didn't have legs and thinking instead, *How can I find this treasure?*

Cheerleading, not treasure, was on my mind 24-7—even while I was talking to the tourists. I couldn't wait until I got off work and could meet up with my team. When summer ended my job went back to being part-time, leaving time for cheerleading practice, which we did every day after school. All of us on the squad were becoming good friends and throughout the fall we worked together to come up with routines and moves.

The others especially liked having me on the squad because I was small and light, and even the girls got a kick out of seeing me cartwheel across the gym. It was like being part of a family.

In the weeks leading up to the cheerleading state championships, I found myself becoming more and more distracted during classes—except, of course, for Ms. Jasper's mythology course. I would wake up at six a.m.—a great challenge as I am a night person, *definitely not* a morning person—head to school and practise with the squad until the bell rang for first period. After school, I would bounce from cheerleading practice to drama club to home to study for my math and English midterm exams. It was a demanding schedule.

As hard as I tried, Debbie refused to let me do what we call in cheerleading the basket-toss. This was when three people would throw me up in the air. While in the air I would do a somersault, and then I'd be caught by the three people who threw me. The team thought we had the best chance of perfectly executing this move at the competition since I weighed, on my heavy days, no more than seventy-five pounds.

But alas, it couldn't happen.

"Spencer," Debbie said, peering out from her big, wire-rimmed glasses, "the state says they don't have insurance should you be dropped. You see, if the person who is being thrown loses their balance or is dropped during the catch, their instinct is to land on their legs or bum. You, because you don't have legs, would land on your back and risk a spinal injury. I'm sorry," she said, giving me a hug. "I know you wanted to do this."

In the end, however, it didn't matter. "Team," Debbie began before we went out on the stadium floor during the state competition. "You have worked really hard for this. You know the routine, so just go out there and have fun!"

And I did. Like a flash, all the good parts of my life hit me— my family, my friends, my work, my life! I was happy to be alive.

When the main Casper television station interviewed me after the performance, the energy of what I had just done was still pulsing through me.

"If I want to do something," I told the announcer, "I do it. I will always find a way to do it!"

That flash of connectedness that I felt during the cheerleading competition lasted and lasted. Our cheerleading squad returned to Rock Springs, elated and full of pride to have represented our school so well. I was on top of the world.

Not long after that, I learned I had received a small scholarship for college. And shortly after that, my acceptance letter for Westminster College in Salt Lake City arrived in the mail. The idea of Westminster appealed to me for it was a small, private college, in a city I was familiar with from both my hospital days and having frequently visited Marci.

Knowing what the next year held for me, I relaxed and threw myself into my final role in drama club, the nerd in *The Yearbook*. Just before our performance was prom and, of course, Marci was my date. She wore an elegant, strapless gold ball gown and I wore a black tuxedo jacket with a flaming red waistcoat and tie. I also aced my final exams. Then, on graduation day, I discovered I had won the award for most outstanding student, which was selected by the faculty. When I went up to accept my plaque, the entire graduating class gave me a standing ovation. I remember thinking afterward that some of those standing were kids who had bullied me and my friends all through high school, or at least made us feel like outsiders. Maybe Marci's Mom was right when she said that by college all of the "it" people would be more mature and nice. No matter. It was a powerful feeling to be recognized by my classmates.

The night after graduation, Mom hosted a big party for me, attended by my friends and family. Like at all my family's gatherings, there was a smorgasbord of delights from around the world: Greek pastries, Italian pastas with homemade sauce, sausage from Boschetto's deli, cabbage rolls and cold cuts. Dad and Grandpa Callas were making wine by then, using Greatgrandpa Corona's original formula. It flowed through the house that night, so much so that a usually reserved Grandpa Callas donned a grass skirt and Hawaiian hat and did the Macarena. John, Marci and I left the celebration halfway through to go to the senior party. This was an all-night celebration put on by the high school Grade 12 parents—and the last night all of us in Grade 12 would be together.

A couple weeks later, John, Marci and I headed to New York City with Mr. Kellar, some members of the drama club and some other students. Growing up, my family didn't take a lot of vacations. For one, Dad always worked. And Mom, when Annie and I were in school full-time, began working as well, eventually landing a position with the school board, first as a secretary for a high school principal and then as executive secretary to the superintendent of schools. Our family holidays were usually spent at Grandpa West's cabin or visiting my aunt Jamie, who moved to Casper, Wyoming, when Uncle Phillip finished medical school. We also made a few trips to visit my aunts Tammy and Diana and their daughters Bonnie and Desi, all living in Arizona. Tammy worked for Arizona State University as the registrar for the law department and Diana was an engineer for the telephone company Qwest Communications. Going to South Africa with Grandpa West and my Dad was my first trip overseas. And New York City was my first trip without my family, something that was a big deal then.

Anyway, when we arrived in New York I plopped myself down on one twin bed in the room John and I shared at the hotel. I closed my eyes and revelled in the city sounds coming in through the open window: taxi drivers honking their horns, ambulance sirens, babies crying, children laughing, adults arguing in languages I didn't understand. I breathed in the smog and cigarette smoke from the streets below. I felt my cotton T-shirt sticking to my back and arms from the humidity in the air. Wyoming is dry, never humid, and we rarely, if ever, have traffic. Birds chirping, wind blowing, Dad telling hunting stories—that's Rock Springs.

I felt alive and also invisible on the streets of New York City. No one even looked at me, let alone said hello, which I liked. It seemed like everyone in Rock Springs knew me, knew my story, knew when I had pimples, knew when I got braces, knew when Patrick pulled my wheelchair out from underneath me. "Everyone in Rock Springs knows everyone else's business," John would lament, waving his hands and playing with his spiked, overly gelled red hair. "We've gotta get out of Rock Springs!" was a common statement.

And he would. He had always dreamed of being an architect, designing high-rises. When we were in high school, he used to design buildings in class, including a skyscraper he said would be mine one day. On the front of the building, John had put my initials: S.J.W. And while we were in New York City, he dragged Marci and me along to look at the Chrysler Building and the Empire State Building. Well, John got his wish. He was accepted into the architecture program at the University of Wyoming. And Marci, who liked to look after others, was accepted into the nursing program at Truman State University in Missouri. "We're getting out! We're getting out!" John and Marci chanted when their acceptance letters arrived in the mail.

New York City was our first taste of real freedom. We went to two Broadway plays—*Beauty and the Beast* and *Les Misérables*. I sang, "Do you hear the people sing? Singing a song of angry men? It is the music of a people who will not be slaves again!" all the way to our hotel after *Les Mis*. I stopped only when I found myself on a subway grate for the very first time in my life. A subway car passed underneath, sending a rush of hot air up at me. I felt like I was Marilyn Monroe *sans* the white skirt. "Do you hear the people sing?" I continued.

I bought a shiny shirt in Soho. Marci dyed her blonde hair

blue, and John and I got our ears pierced. We ate New York–style pizza, the kind with the thin crust that you fold in half to eat. "I am so going to come back here," I told myself that night, as John and I jumped on our beds. "I am going to be a *star!* I'm going to be like Barbara Streisand on Broadway, or maybe even sing at Madison Square Garden."

I then closed my eyes, tilted my head up to the sky and sang Barbara Streisand's "A Piece of Sky," from the movie *Yentl.* (Mom had rented it years earlier, and I'd listened to the soundtrack over and over and over):

Tell me where
Where is it written?
What it is I'm meant to be?
That I can't dare...

Ms. Jasper's mythology class taught me that the hero's journey is rarely linear. The hero's rise from their initial wound or challenge is seldom steady. There are peaks and valleys—high tides and low tides, as Ms. Jasper likes to call them.

I knew what I wanted: for that wonderful, elated, optimistic feeling from the cheerleading championship and my trip to New York to last. I just assumed the feeling would sustain itself, and I didn't think it would involve much effort on my part. Nor did I understand that the optimistic attitude I'd adopted early on in life, my ability to twist and turn my way through obstacles, had been the labor that brought about the reward of that great feeling in the first place.

And so, unknowingly, I was setting myself up for a crash landing.

It started after I returned home from New York, when my Mom suggested that I study something other than theater at college. "Spencer, I understand your love for acting, but you need to be realistic," she said. "What if acting doesn't work out and you have nothing to fall back on? Please think about studying something else, as I would hate to see you struggle."

I pleaded with Mom and reminded her about Greatgrandpa Corona, who had risked it all to move to the United States from Italy, just to be an accordion player.

"I am not saying I don't want you to act. Quite the contrary. I do," Mom replied. "But I also think you should major in something else, something that would help you with a career outside the performing arts, just in case. Remember, Grandpa Corona spent his life working in the coal mines to support his family, even though his music was his art and passion."

I felt so letdown. I had a path that I knew I wanted to go down.

"You can always do what you did at high school, Spencer," she continued. "You can join the drama club and do theater on the side." And so that is how I decided to study computer science, as I had loved my classes and work with Mr. Biedschied, back in middle school.

I was excited to attend Westminster College. It was far enough away from Rock Springs for me to be independent and have my own life and identity, but close enough that I could come home on weekends. I was one of few students in my graduating class going to Westminster, which I liked as well. "I just don't want the cliques and gossip to follow me," I told John and Marci. "I'm ready to get out of this town and make some new friends."

Marci, John and our friends Phillip and Starr had a good-bye party at Starr's house the night before I was to leave for Salt Lake City. We had chocolate cake, listened to music and strolled down memory lane, retelling some of our favorite memories from Rock Springs. (The four of us, for example, went to our first concert together—to see Alanis Morissette in Salt Lake City.)

At midnight, we turned to each other to say goodbye. Starr, who is model gorgeous, with her tall, slim body and flaming red hair, gave me a big hug, lifting me high off the ground. My tears came quickly, and I was still crying when I hugged John and then Marci. And I was still crying when I got in the van and started driving Phillip home. I pulled onto Rock Springs' main street and I didn't even hear the siren, I was so distracted by my grief. It was the police car's flashing lights in the rear-view mirror that finally got my attention.

I was being pulled over.

The police officer shined his flashlight on me and his anger about me going over the speed limit changed to concern. "Son, what is the matter? Are you OK?"

I choked, but managed to get out: "I'm OK. I'm leaving for college tomorrow. I was saying goodbye to my friends."

He went to his squad car and returned with a written warning for me to slow down. On the bottom of the ticket in blue ink were the words: "Good luck in school!"

Chapter 8

The next day, I headed to Salt Lake City. I drove my van, packed to the brim with my computer, a television and suitcases full of clothes, bedding and boxes of food. Mom, Dad, Annie, Grandma and Grandpa Callas, Aunt Jamie, Uncle Phillip and their two children, Mitchell and Emily, met me there. The college had given me a room in one of the new campus residences, an apartment-style complex simply called Residence Hall 4. At that time, Residence Hall 4 was one of the only residences at the school that was wheelchair accessible. My apartment was on the first floor and I would share the kitchen, living room and two bathrooms with four other students. My roommates were in second and third year so they didn't have to show up for another week. As a freshman, I had to be at the university a week early for orientation.

The college told Mom and Dad not to linger; to say their

goodbyes quickly in order to allow me to settle in. So after my clothes were put away in the closet and dressers, my cups, plates and cutlery tucked away in the cupboards and drawers, the potica cookies Mom, Jamie and Grandma Callas had baked to snack on and my computer set up, everyone wished me good luck and left.

The advice of the university administrators for my family to depart harkened back to my first days in Salt Lake City, when doctors and nurses forbade Mom and Dad from spending the night with me in the hospital. As Mom left, she had tears in her eyes. When the door was closed and I was left alone in my quiet apartment, I too cried. I felt alone and afraid. It was an eerie feeling and one that I had felt before. My telephone and cable had not been set up yet, so I couldn't call anyone or distract myself by watching television. I eventually lied down in bed and went to sleep early.

And so my depression began.

The high I had been riding ended, abruptly. I felt as if I was falling off a steep mountain—desperately trying to hang on, mind you—but I was spiralling my way down, nonetheless.

A few days after my arrival at Westminster, all of the freshmen headed to a welcome retreat in the tall, majestic mountains of Utah. I met a few students, but no one who I clicked with right away. When I returned back to my apartment, I met my roommates. To my astonishment, they didn't seem to be surprised upon discovering I had no legs. Occasionally, over time, they would ask me questions like how I ended up ... the way I ended up. They were amazed I could get around as easily as I could. Mostly, however, they left me alone. We lived our own, separate lives. Two of the guys were on the basketball team and rarely ever at the apartment. One of them was engaged and would leave midterm to live with his soon-to-be wife. My other roommate was into grunge music, left his room messy, grunted hellos and was rarely seen. The roommate who joined us midterm, replacing the basketball player who left, was devotedly Mormon.

Most of the students at the school were Mormon and members of the Church of Jesus Christ of Latter-day Saints. Many knew each other from church. Many were in serious relationships and announcing their engagements, or looking for serious relationships in the hopes of announcing their engagements. It seemed to me that having a social life at Westminster meant dating. And I wasn't quite there yet. As Mom once said to me: "Spencer, you are different and it might take you a little bit longer to find that special person."

My classes were challenging, too. The readings, assignments and tests were never-ending, from trigonometry to U.S. history. In some courses, I just couldn't keep up. I would walk past the bulletin boards announcing theater tryouts or plays being performed on campus and hang my head. "There is no way I can go out," I told Mom when I went home one weekend. "I just have too much to do." My true passions were being blocked.

It was on one of these weekends home that John and I had a falling out over some argument he was having with Phillip.

That was a hard day, having our friendship come to an abrupt halt. Losing a friend, especially a close friend that was by your side for all of high school, is a hard blow. My falling out with Marci was more gradual.

"Hey Spence," I heard when she called me one rainy afternoon in mid-fall. "How is Westminster?" Before I could reply, however, she started talking to me about her life and filling me in on all the parties she was going to, the people she was meeting and the great marks she was getting in her program. Then it was all over. She never gave me a chance to talk about what I was experiencing. I didn't have the chance to let her know how I was feeling.

And things were going from terrible to worse. My midterms came in and I was getting C's, D's and an F in computer science, which was supposed to be my major. Like at the beginning of White Mountain Junior High, I was eating almost all of my meals at a table full of strangers, and other times completely alone. But unlike at White Mountain, my solitude at Westminster stretched into months. I wasn't meeting anyone. I was alone without my family or close friends to fall back on.

I drove myself home on a snowy day just before Christmas, sullen and failing computer science. Halfway to Rock Springs I made a decision: "I am going to tell Mom that I want to quit. I'm going to take next semester off and apply to a new college for the following September."

Mom, of course, wasn't receptive to the idea.

"Spencer, you need to give Westminster a full year. Then, if you want to change colleges, you can. But you need to give it a chance. Not everything falls into your lap as quickly or as neatly as you'd like." Before I even had time to digest this information, Mom dealt me another blow: "By the way, Spencer, I too have been thinking. I don't want you coming home as much next term." Mom was speaking about my almost weekly, certainly bimonthly trips back to Rock Springs. "Next term, come home maybe once a month," she said. "You need to try and make some friends and you need to study harder, to find what it is you want to do. We will get you a tutor for computers, but think about changing your major, before changing your college."

"Stop feeling sorry for yourself," she added. "That is the reason you are not making any friends."

Her response definitely caught me off guard as I had hoped she would sympathize and tell me to come home. But slowly, as the days wore on, I realized my mother was right, as mothers typically are.

Two nights after Christmas dinner, Marci, visiting Rock Springs from Missouri, came by my house. She jumped on my bed and picked up exactly where her phone conversations left off. She started going on and on about how much fun she was having at Truman State. I patiently listened. When she was done, I exploded.

"Marci, you haven't given me a chance to answer any of your questions about how I'm liking school. Every time we talk," I said, raising my voice, "it is all about you." I was almost screaming. "I hate school. I am *not* having fun. I have no friends and I am failing the subject I'm supposed to be majoring in. You abandoned me!"

After I was finished, silence filled the room. Then, in a calm and quiet voice, Marci replied: "If you don't want to be friends anymore, I understand." She started to tremble and broke into tears. It was the first time in my entire life I had ever seen Marci cry. She was my rock. She was the strong one that held John and me together. Watching her cry made me feel numb.

Marci sat on my bed for several minutes and then got up and abruptly left. She was gone for about thirty minutes. When she came back, she said: "You've really grown up. I had no idea, Spence. I never meant to hurt you. I've been a bad friend lately. I'm sorry."

I looked up at her tear-stained face and said spitefully: "I know. Everyone left me. I didn't have a choice!"

Marci left after that. I didn't walk her out. I didn't say good-bye. In my mind, our friendship was over.

A few days after New Year's, I drove back to Salt Lake City feeling more alone than I ever had in my life. It was the same, deep feeling of loneliness that I first encountered during my surgeries. Those times that I cried myself to sleep without my Mom. I thought to myself, *I have no friends and I'm flunking school. What am I going to do?*

I entered the dark night of my soul.

Or, as Alanis Morissette sings in "Precious Illusions," which would become one of my favorite songs in years to come:

These precious illusions in my head did not let me down when I was a kid, and parting with them is like parting with a childhood best friend.

Except in my case, I really did lose all of my childhood best friends. And unlike when I started White Mountain, there were no friends on the horizon ready to ease the transition to my new life as a college student. All I had was a song and some subpar grades. Yipee.

My academic counsellor found me a tutor for computer science. But no matter how hard I tried, I just couldn't sink my teeth into the course material. "It will eventually click," my tutor, Alfie, would say patiently in his soft voice. But it never did. The only happiness I found for much of that January of my freshman year was watching *The Rosie O'Donnell Show*. I was there, in my room, at three p.m. every day, glued to the television set. I watched Rosie learn to cook with Joan Lunden, flirt with Tom Cruise and sing with Barbara Streisand.

It was after that last show that I wheeled myself over to the window and looked out.

Night had fallen early, it being midwinter. I watched two female students in brightly colored scarves having a snowball fight with a red-haired young man. I thought of my red-haired John, and then Marci, and the snowball fights we had back home in Rock Springs. I found myself singing Alanis's song "Precious Illusions" again. This time, I kept getting stuck on one line: "I've spent so long firmly looking outside me."

"That's it," I said to myself. "Every hero, on his mythic journey, needs to go *inward*."

I wheeled myself to my computer and began searching websites for information on Joseph Campbell's idea of the hero's journey. One site listed a summary of the steps the hero takes, with the first being the "call to adventure." I realized that was what happened to me with cheerleading, and then again in New York. The call to adventure.

"Oh, geez," I gasped aloud, as I read the descriptions of some of the other steps. "I am right in the middle of the hero's journey."

I became so engrossed in my reading that I completely missed dinner that night. At about midnight, I shut off the computer, lay down on my bed and contemplated everything.

I was at the stages that Campbell calls "refusing the call" and "in the belly of the whale." I knew, for example, that I wanted to do theater of some sort. I wanted to entertain people. But I had let my depression stop me from even *going* to a play on campus. I had refused the call. I'd let obstacles hold me back.

"In the belly of the whale" is the point in the hero's journey when he or she is transiting between worlds and selves. I, of course, was moving from Rock Springs and my comfortable, sheltered life to having to take responsibility for myself and my own happiness. Mom was right, like usual. I needed to stop feeling sorry for myself. I needed to fight for what I wanted.

One small problem: everything around me showed me what I *didn't* want.

Before falling asleep, I racked my brain, reliving memories of my past, summing up those moments when I was truly at peace with myself, and asking myself the same question over and over again: "What is it I am meant to do in life? What is the adventure I am being called to take?" I came up with nothing but I knew that it was time I faced my fears and looked inside myself.

When the hero eventually lets go and surrenders to his or her journey, something magical begins to happen. Campbell calls it the stage of "supernatural aid." This guiding force may not be visible at first, and it is only now, in looking back, that I fully see that something greater than me was at work. But slowly, as I began to learn to be alone, really alone, people—or as I call them now, *my angels*—started to emerge.

It all started with a phone call from Marci.

"Hey, kid," she said, timidly. "How ... how are you doing?" This time, I reached out to her too. I said I was not doing so well. And we talked, albeit briefly, and she wished me much love and happiness and hoped I met some new friends quickly.

Soon enough I met Corinne, a third-year student. In my second term I decided to take a course I knew I could ace—Spanish, which I had studied in Grades 9 and 10. Corinne and I met in the cafeteria, when we were both standing in line to check out our trays of food. I was carrying my Spanish textbook. *"Hola! Cómo estás?"* she said, eyeing the book. While eating our salads, she and I spoke Spanish, which was her major. Just as she was getting up to leave, she asked: "A friend of mine and I go Latin dancing every Friday night. Do you want to join us?"

I sure did. *Anything to get me out of the apartment,* I thought.

We had a good time, and bonded quickly over our love of the Spanish language and anything Latin, from the merengue to Ricky Martin, quesadillas to salsa. We started going to Latin clubs once a month or so, and I liked the reprieve from being on campus.

I would go to the nightclubs in my wheelchair, but dance on my hands. Often my friends would circle around me when we headed out to the dance floor, as these typically are busy places. Because I was tiny, they were afraid I would get stepped on by other patrons, so I was usually in the middle, doing my rendition of the salsa or the flamenco on my hands. No one at the nightclubs ever bothered me. I think they were really quite impressed that I was there, and had a couple dance moves up my sleeve.

Then another angel emerged. I returned from a solitary dinner in the cafeteria one night to find an e-mail in my inbox from Dan. Dan was a year older and also from Rock Springs. He had been in *The Music Man* with me and in some of my choir classes. Dan, who was tall and stocky, had dreams of becoming an opera star, singing the part of Figaro in *The Barber of Seville* or "La Donna è Mobile" from *Rigoletto* by Verdi at the Met. He was struggling too, as he wrote in his e-mail, taking on a string of low-paying jobs in retail and construction. "BUT I AM IN SALT LAKE CITY," he wrote in capital letters. "I moved here a year ago and I just heard you are here, too. We should hang out." Two days after that, Dan popped by my apartment to use my computer then we headed to my residence's basement to play some pool and ping pong. Dan and I started going to movies. As a result I started to feel less lonely.

And then I reconnected with my original dream. Well, sort of.

Erin, a dark-haired girl in one of my classes, learned I had been a cheerleader. "You should join us!" she pleaded with me, referring to the group taking morning classes at the campus dance studio. Westminster had only just started a sports program, which included a basketball team. Erin and some of her friends had started a dance squad to dance before and during the half times of the games.

"We just, well—we're new," she explained. "And we're not that organized. But we would love to have you."

It was nice to feel wanted, so I said: "OK, I'll try."

The very next day, and from then on for about a month, I managed to get myself to the dance studio by six a.m., wearing my pajamas, a sweatshirt and a baseball cap. Along with the others brave enough to come out at that hour in the morning, I learned a routine to Will Smith's "Wild Wild West." Just like when I first turned out to cheerleading practice, the dancers seemed to love my being involved. They included me. They laughed with me, and we bonded. We were all there at such an early hour, dedicated to doing our best!

A month later, we decided we were ready for the basketball court. We were—and we did great. But there was no one there. Sports were so new at Westminster, there were hardly any spectators in the stands. The music echoed across the deserted gymnasium.

I quit going to dance class soon after because of my course

work, but I was not disappointed. I enjoyed my month of being a dancer, and it reminded me how much I loved the performing arts, and how much I'd missed being a part of that kind of creative work. I performed on my hands, like I had as a cheerleader. I loved it and for a while I started to feel what I felt when I was on the cheerleading squad back in Rock Springs—a sense of belonging, being part of something, having a purpose. For the few months I did dance, I loved every moment of it. But dance wasn't my passion, as I soon discovered. And I had more important things to think about—final exams.

Yes, my course work was heavy, so much so that I had started skipping computer science class to keep up with the classes that at least I had a chance of passing, like Spanish and photography. Exams were now looming and I had decided to not write my computer science exam. My academic counsellor told me matter-of-factly that not only would I fail the course, I'd lose my scholarship. But I knew it was too late—there was no way I could pass the class, even if I aced the test.

Mom was sympathetic when I told her I wasn't going to take the final exam, and what the ramifications would be.

"We're disappointed, but if that is what is going to happen, that is what will happen," she said.

Marci tried to cheer me up as well. "That sucks. It will be hard to get your GPA up. But you have to do something you want to do," she said during one of our now biweekly telephone conversations. She started encouraging me to move to Los Angeles and take a stab at acting.

When I was alone at night I had moments of true panic. My body would pulsate, my breathing would become erratic and I wanted to explode. For the first time in my life I had failed. This was something I had never experienced before and there was no one to blame but myself, which made me feel even worse. Crazy thoughts kept going through my head like, the only way I could succeed at anything was to rely on help from others. I had wanted so badly to prove to the world that, despite everything, I could succeed independently, and yet here I was losing my scholarship. I was instantly brought back to the days of being alone in the hospital, but now I was completely alone and my parents wouldn't be there in the morning.

Failure had visited me, but I soon learned it wouldn't last long.

Just before I was scheduled to drive back to Rock Springs to work at the Chamber of Commerce tourism center for the summer, another dose of magic came my way. Aunt Tammy, upon hearing that I had failed computer science, called to tell me about this really cool degree program at Arizona State University called mass media. "You can take theater, journalism, writing, broadcast—mass media combines all these disciplines. What about seeing if Westminster has a course like that?" she asked.

It was too late for me to change to Arizona State. I was stuck at Westminster for at least another year. I had to choose a new major.

I wheeled myself into my counsellor's office the very next day and told her about Aunt Tammy and the course she talked about at Arizona. Westminster didn't have mass media, she told me, but did have something called communications, a degree program that combined some of those same classes. She opened her laptop and began looking at the course requirements for Westminster's communications program. She then compared my marks to what was needed to get in.

I started to twiddle my thumbs. She frowned, I frowned. I thought I was done for. After a long silence, she finally spoke. "I think you'll be OK," she replied. "Kept you in suspense, didn't I?" She winked. "But I think you will be more than OK."

I smiled.

We went over the courses I would have to take that fall: writing for mass media, layout and design, marketing and advertising. "And you can take an elective, too," she finally beamed. "Like ... theater!"

"No!" I exclaimed.

"Yes," she laughed.

If my residence hall wasn't at the other end of the campus, I would have skipped (on my hands) back to my apartment. Life wasn't just looking up, it was great. The minute I got back to my room I called my Mom and then Aunt Jamie to tell them the news, both of whom were extremely excited for me. During the conversation, Aunt Jamie said, "Spencer, I am so sorry. I thought computer science would be ideal for you, because you could pull your wheelchair up to a desk and work. But I was completely wrong. You have always been a people person and need to be interacting with others, not stuck behind a desk somewhere. Communication seems like the perfect fit."

I packed up my van after that and headed home for summer holidays. All in all, my freshman year of college had been good. I know, I know, how can metaphorically sitting on a razor blade be looked at positively? But in my freshman year, I learned to surrender and I learned that it is OK to be alone. I also learned that when I let go of things, what comes back to me may not be what I want, but certainly is what I need—like the friends I found, and how Aunt Tammy helped me find a program that resonated far better with who I was as a person. On the sunny drive back to Rock Springs, I began to dream of my future. Maybe I could be a broadcaster on television or host a radio show—*a morning Top 40 show*. Communications was a perfect way for me to do what Mom asked me to do—get a degree in something other than theater, and follow my heart while I was at it.

Mom, Dad, Annie and I spent several weekends that summer at the cabin. One Wednesday my Mom asked me if there was anyone I wanted to invite. "Annie is bringing a friend, why don't you?" she asked.

I didn't know who to invite. Phillip worked on the weekends. Marci was spending the summer in Kansas City. And John—he was home in Rock Springs, but we were still not talking.

I must have stared at that telephone for half an hour before I got the courage to pick up the receiver.

"John," I said, when he answered. "It's Spencer."

"Hi," he said. I could hear the shock in his voice.

"Hey, we're going to the cabin this weekend. Do you want to come?" I asked.

There was a short silence on the telephone, and then John said sure.

It was just like old times. We went tubing behind Grandpa West's motorboat. We drove the four-wheeler through the roads in the mountains, and we told ghost stories with Annie and her friend in the loft at night. When Annie and her friend were asleep, John told me about being in Laramie at the University of Wyoming.

"You could just feel the pressure in the city during the trial for Matthew Shepard's killers," he said. "You know one of Matthew's murderers pleaded guilty. The other was convicted. But Matthew's father asked for the death penalty to be taken off the table. Can you believe it? His Dad said something like, 'I give you life, when you did not give my son life. I give you life and hope so that every Thanksgiving, Christmas and birthday, you think of the life you have taken. I give you life.' Oh, I'm not sure of his exact words." John sighed and lay back on his pillow.

"You know I am gay, Spence," he finally said. "And being in Laramie during Matthew Shepard's trial was really difficult. It made me dig deep, find myself and then study the history of who I am, to arm myself against the hate. I am proud to be who I am."

"I'm proud of you, too," I whispered. And I was.

While I knew I had been spending most of that year alone, I discovered that weekend that John was on his own soul-searching journey—and one that he had to embark upon alone. That year was one of the most painful for me, yet in the end it was becoming one of the most rewarding. Like John, I, too, was learning a lot about myself—and I was discovering, among other things, who my friends really were.

Chapter 9

I slipped into my sophomore year at college far more relaxed than the year before. I lived in the dorms again, but this time I got to choose my roommates. There was Rick, a good friend of Corrine's, and Don, who was part of the theater program and the residence representative for our floor. We were all very similar in our personalities; we all liked musical theater, for instance. We were having fun. My course work was also great. I loved every class, and by midterms my marks were right about where they had been in high school—A's and a few B's. I felt like I could breathe again.

So when midterms were over, and my studying schedule had taken on a manageable rhythm, I decided to look for something to do on the side.

Since I was fourteen, I'd earned my own pocket money, starting out by filing at Grandma Callas's real estate agency. I loved working. I also enjoyed having extra money for great clothes. So I decided to get a part-time job.

I spent an evening putting my résumé together and, one Monday in between classes, I headed out to the shopping malls. I applied to several of the hipper clothing stores in Salt Lake City, including Old Navy. I didn't hear back from anyone. I called several of the stores. Left messages. Called them again. Finally, after showing up twice and enquiring as to the status of my application, the hiring manager at Old Navy called me, one evening in late fall. "Can you come in for an interview? We are looking for seasonal help."

I got the job, which involved selling, working the cash desk and running the fitting rooms. I was part of a team of extra help hired for the store's busiest times, weeknights and weekends starting in mid-November, leading up to U.S. Thanksgiving at the end of the month and the Christmas shopping that followed. I drove my van through the rains and then snows of Salt Lake City three times a week to the mall where the Old Navy was located and made enough cash to pay for all of my extracurricular activities, like going to the movies. I bought everyone in the family Old Navy clothes for Christmas presents that year, too, which helped the wallet.

Closing was the best time of the day. The doors were locked and all of us would stay behind, sometimes as long as an hour, folding clothes, blasting the music and singing along. One night, Tina Turner's "Proud Mary" came on and a young woman named Jessica and I belted out the lyrics while standing on the counter re-enacting the dance moves.

"You know, you are *good,*" Leslie, one of the store managers, said to me. "Have you ever thought of performing on stage?"

I wheeled over beside her and, as we folded sweatshirts, I told her all about my past theater experience. Near the end of our conversation, she said: "Well, my ex-husband Roland and I are professional dancers and choreographers. We did the choreography for the movie *Footloose,* which was filmed outside Salt Lake City. Roland is currently doing the choreography for *No, No, Nanette* at Salt Lake Community College and he's desperately looking for young men to be in the ensemble. You should look into it."

My eyes widened. "Yes!" I replied, exuberant. "Where? When? NOW!"

Leslie laughed and scribbled down the address of where the cast was rehearsing. "I'll let Roland know that you're interested."

Roland was indeed short of men who could sing, and I didn't even need to try out for the production. But *No, No, Nanette* is a musical with lots of dancing. Sure, I had danced with Amber in Grade 6. And the high school production of *The Music Man* had me twirling around in my wheelchair at certain moments to match the songs we were singing. But *No, No, Nanette* involved *tap* dancing. To my surprise, however, Roland didn't hesitate at all in asking me to get out of my wheelchair and do some numbers on stage along with the other men and also dancing in my chair tapping my wheels as the ensemble tapped their shoes.

No, No, Nanette originally debuted in London, England, in

1925. It is a story of a blackmail scheme, a woman named Nanette desperately trying to break free and find herself, and three couples at a cottage in Atlantic City. It's most known for its breakout hit, "Tea for Two." The director of the play gave me speaking lines; Roland taught me to dance. One dance sequence included me doing the can-can in my wheelchair and a floor routine dressed in old-fashioned swimming garb.

No, No, Nanette was my very first professional gig. I practised non-stop, singing my lines in my van on the way to Old Navy, in my room alone before bed, even at dinners with Dan. Dan, too, was starting to sink his teeth into fulfilling his own dreams. He had been accepted into the Utah Opera Company, so we supported each other.

Performing in *No, No, Nanette* was one of the standout experiences of my life. Roland and the other members of the cast became family—my Salt Lake City family. And out of *No, No, Nanette* came my second professional gig. I was asked to play the part of Barnaby Tucker in an outdoor theater production of *Hello, Dolly!* that very same summer. It was a busy time.

But I am fast-forwarding here.

After the Christmas holidays, Leslie and the rest of the management at Old Navy asked me to stay on. My seasonal position became a permanent part-time job that I did until I graduated from Westminster. And it was while I was on duty on a snowy January day in 2002 that another angel walked— sorry—sauntered into my life, like a movie star.

Reed Cowan, the morning host for the Salt Lake City ABC affiliate, ABC 4, came in when I was on duty, looking for jeans for his then two-year-old son, Wesley. Reed ended up in my section, looking for a pair for himself.

Fielding calls on my headset from the assistant manager, and with the music of Bob Marley's "Sun is Shining" playing in the background, I helped Reed find his size and then wheeled along beside him to the change room. I then took the jeans he wanted to purchase to the cashier, shook Reed's hand and left to help another customer.

I had no idea, at the time, that I had just helped one of Salt Lake City's top celebrities. One of my coworkers quickly filled me in. "Do you know who that was?" she asked, one of her hands over her mouth in shock.

"No," I said and then, picking up on her star-stuck demeanour, added: "Brad Pitt?"

She laughed and explained. "No, he's the cutest guy on the news—Reed Cowan! He's won lots of awards, and he's just so dreamy!"

"OK," I replied, amused.

Two days later, Leslie handed me a slip of paper. Reed had been back, looking for me. "He left this for you," Leslie hummed. The note read:

Hello Spencer,

I work for ABC 4. Please call the station when you have a moment. I would like to meet you again. -Reed

The first thing I said when I got Reed on the telephone was: "I believe you've made a mistake. You want to meet me again?

Are you sure it isn't someone else at Old Navy?"

Reed laughed and then asked if he could be direct with me.

"Yes, of course," I replied.

Reed explained that when he had met me, he was having a very, very bad day.

"And then you leapt out of your wheelchair, with that Old Navy headset on, smiling, no, just beaming. You moved from one display to another, pulling out jeans and T-shirts, and tossing them into my arms. My dark, dark day changed in an instant," he said. "On that day I was so low, I had no frame of reference on life. My problems seemed huge, and here you were walking on your hands and working at Old Navy. You gave me a moment of perspective, showing that you can shine through your troubles and you can overcome anything. I would like to do a television news segment on you."

How could I say no after a declaration like that?

Reed and I met up again a few days later. By that point I had moved off campus. I had become so comfortable being alone during my freshman year that I decided halfway through my sophomore year to get my own place. So I showed Reed around the tiny apartment I'd rented in the center of Salt Lake City. Then we sat in the kitchen and I told him my about my life.

At the end, Reed was thrilled with my story. "And you clean, too. Your place is so tidy."

"No," I laughed. "My grandmother Callas pays for a cleaning lady to come two times a month." I then added: "I'm pretty boring. I don't think anyone is going to want to watch a news story about me."

"I disagree," Reed replied, eyeing me closely. He shifted from foot to foot. "I don't know you that well, yet, but I'm a pretty intuitive man. I feel three things: I am going to do a show on you that will inspire lots of people. You and I will become good—no, great—friends. And one day, I bet, you will be a public speaker."

"No, perform on stage, maybe," I replied. "But who would ever want to hear me speak? I have nothing to say." I knew that I'd amazed people in the past with my cheerleading and my theater work—people who wouldn't have expected someone without legs to be able to do all of that, but I'd become used to that reaction.

"You wait and see," he said. Then he left, only to reappear a few days later with a camera crew that followed me around for a day.

"Overcoming Adversity" was the name of the segment that aired about me on ABC Channel 4 one morning in the late spring of 2002. Reed had Mom send him photographs dating all the way back to when I was a baby.

"Great pain accompanies greater perspective," Reed said in his narration, referring to me. "He turned stumbling blocks into stepping stones. See him for what is on the inside and when life is down, look up."

At the end of the segment, Reed had me live in the studio sitting beside him and his co-anchor. Reed asked me a few questions and then let me lead the station into the break: "Coming up on *Good Morning Utah*..."

At some point during our time together, I asked Reed if his

station ever offered student internships. "Of course," he said. And not long after the segment on me aired, Reed invited me to the studio to meet the radio staff, including the disc jockeys, and that was where I garnered my first media job. As an intern at the radio station I wrote public service announcements and organized the prize closet.

After the radio job, I moved on to an internship at the television show *Good Things Utah*. I was a production assistant. Translation: a gopher. And I wasn't going to let the fact I was in a wheelchair prevent me from doing anything the other interns could do. I carried dishes from the on-air kitchen to the kitchen where we actually cleaned them during the food segments. I got up on the counter and scrubbed those pots and pans. I was also the liaison for the guests who came in, making sure they had water, coffee, tea, cookies and tours of the station.

All the while, Reed and I were becoming good friends, just like he'd predicted. He became my mentor, and at every opportunity told me that I was going to be a star one day. Not for my own sake, but for others.

After my sophomore year—in which I took two drama classes as my electives, and my roles in *No, No, Nanette* and *Hello, Dolly!*—I felt confident to approach the heads of the drama department on campus, a couple named Michael and Nina, and asked to join. My first big role was as a Gollum-like creature in the play *The Illusion* by Tony Kushner. I crept out of a mist generated by a fog machine, and Michael had rigged a contraption that, at one point, made me grow larger than life on a pair of stilts, creating the illusion that I had legs.

When not rehearsing or performing in the school play, I was learning how to write in a journalistic style in my communications courses. Eventually I could zing off an Associated Press-worthy story about the happenings in Utah quicker than anyone, and there was a lot to write about. For one, the Winter Olympics came to Salt Lake City when I was in my third year. I didn't get to see any of the actual events, but I saw the Olympic cauldron every time I drove from my job at Old Navy to my apartment—and every time I got the shivers. *To be on the world stage,* I thought to myself. *What an experience!*

During my fourth and final year at Westminster, I continued to work at Old Navy. My grades were A's and B's at this point. I was interning at ABC. What I wasn't doing was giving a lot of thought as to what I would do when I graduated.

Near the end of that year, Nina and Michael, our drama coaches, held one-on-one meetings with all of the graduating students in the theater club. They were telling us in confidence whether or not we actually had a chance to go professional, and they didn't hold back any punches. When they got to me, Michael said: "Spencer, I think you could make it as an actor. It will be a tough ride. You will have to do a lot of bit roles. But you could make it as a solid sidekick." I liked that—a sidekick. But it wasn't a star.

"We think," Nina concluded, "that you could have a career, an interesting career, but a career nonetheless."

I swallowed hard. They weren't exactly saying I would be a

star, but no one had ever validated that I had real talent before. I went back to my apartment and began strategizing my next moves. Marci was still telling me to move to Los Angeles and slug it out as an actor there. Reed was encouraging me to go into motivational speaking. I was thinking I could make it as a radio or television broadcaster. But where?

I didn't want to stay in Salt Lake City. Los Angeles was too big and I knew no one there. And I didn't want to return to Rock Springs either. Aunt Tammy came up with my answer yet again: Arizona. I loved visiting her and Aunt Diana in Phoenix. My experience was that the city was far more accepting of different people and ideas than Salt Lake City or Rock Springs. I loved the warm, dry air, too, and there was something almost spiritual for me about being there.

Arizona it is, I decided. I would join a community theater company and work for a television station. "And it's a little closer to Los Angeles when I do decide to make the move into full-time acting," I told Marci.

I graduated Westminster on the dean's list. And my résumé was now armed with very solid internships at ABC and to-die-for reference letters from Reed and other ABC staffers. I felt like anything was possible. I was feeling like I did when I first left high school, heading to New York City for the first time.

In the summer of 2003, I finally traded in my blue van for another gently used vehicle—a majestic red Chevy Trailblazer. All I needed to do was install the metal device that allowed me to brake and accelerate with my hands. And in August, my parents hired a moving company to transport my things from

Salt Lake City to Phoenix and we drove down together. The plan was that we would stay with Aunt Tammy for a week, until I moved into the apartment I had rented in the same complex as Aunt Diana. After I was settled, my Mom and Dad would fly home.

When we were about a hundred miles from Phoenix it hit me: I was moving yet again. But unlike when I moved to Salt Lake City, I was just plain excited and pumped about Arizona. The heat hit my face like a hair dryer set to the hottest temperature. I could smell orange blossoms in the air. Phoenix's roads are lined with palm trees, which made me feel like I was somewhere exotic—not in America, but South America. "Enchiladas and tortillas, here I come!" I declared to Dad. Arizona, after all, borders Mexico, and the state is full of authentic Mexican cuisine.

After I moved into my small one-bedroom apartment, which came complete with a swimming pool in the middle of the sprawling complex, Tammy and I came up with a game plan. She would take the next two days off work and drive me around to the television stations. First stop would be the ABC affiliate, where I felt I had the best chance of landing a position.

When I arrived at the television station, I asked the receptionist, a young woman with streaked blonde hair, if I could speak to the hiring manager. "Leave your résumé with me," she said, tapping her long fuchsia nails on the counter.

"Are you sure there isn't any way I could make an appointment to see the manager? I worked at ABC in Salt Lake City," I said. "I have reference letters."

"Good for you, hon," she said, then answered the telephone. After saying hello to whoever was on the line, she cupped her hand over the receiver. "You and every other twenty-two-year-old who passes by my desk have very impressive résumés," she said to me. "But I don't do the hiring. You have to wait for the hiring manager to call you back. Bye-bye now."

I left with my shoulders slumped. This might be tougher than I had thought.

I didn't get much further than that with any of the other stations I visited.

I spent about a month living off my savings from Old Navy, swimming in the pool, dining on Mexican fajitas and faxing, e-mailing and delivering my résumés to every radio and television station within a fifty-mile radius. But no one called me back. Not even the community newspapers.

By then, I couldn't sit around any longer. I had to do something, so I swallowed my pride and went back to retail. For a while I worked in the electronics department at Target, and then for a temp agency, filling a short-term administration position. After that I even worked briefly for an upstart online pharmaceutical company. But I was not cut out for call center work, so after three weeks I quit that job. I needed something permanent. Something that I would enjoy.

Then, one morning about a month later, while sipping on cranberry juice and reading the classified section of the newspaper, an advertisement caught my eye. A new hair salon, called Dolce Salon and Spa, was looking for a receptionist. I knew of Dolce from my visits to the shopping mall. I decided to apply.

A week later, I had a new job.

The owner of Dolce, a twenty-something Arizona socialite named Brandi, explained my duties to me. At the time, she had red, soft hair that she parted to the side. Simply, I was to answer the telephones and book appointments. I could handle this type of call center. I was to call customers for feedback after their appointments and encourage them to pre-book their next visits.

Dolce was always packed with clients, because, in addition to haircuts, the salon provided high-end facials, spa treatments and products that weren't available anywhere else in Phoenix. After a year, Brandi decided to take on another salon. She moved me to a reservation center off-site and gave me a staff, which eventually ballooned to ten.

I realized working at Dolce that I really liked the responsibility of training and managing my own staff. I liked feeling needed, which was further reinforced that first Christmas in Phoenix when my cousin Bonnie decided to get me a dog from the city's humane society as a present. On one of my afternoons off we headed to the kennel, and as soon as I laid eyes on Daisy, a white Beagle mix with chocolate spots, I fell in love. A staff person at the kennel escorted me to a private room and asked if I wanted to see the dog up close. "Yes, please," I said eagerly. There were three of us in the room when she was brought in on shaking legs, at seven months old, but Daisy headed straight to me when she caught my eye. I leapt off my chair and Daisy rushed into my arms, licking my face and eventually toppling me over. Daisy and I became roommates. She even slept with me, nestling her warm body as close to mine as possible for most of the night. ·

The same protectiveness I felt toward Daisy, I felt toward my staff. But I didn't feel that way about the customers who would complain because the water purifier wasn't quite up to their standards or because their streaks of blonde weren't quite light enough and they refused to pay until a stylist fixed it to their liking. I just tried my best to listen patiently and then address their complaints.

Brandi started to set her eyes on a third salon right at the time Annie decided to take a break from her college courses and join me in Arizona. Annie worked for me at the reservation center. We had fun. Especially with the other staff, like Gregg, a half-Asian, half-Mexican young man who wore big chunky gold and silver rings and necklaces over his crisp button down shirts and silk ties. He was over-the-top.

The gossip mill, however, was and still is the misfortune of the industry. Every day I had to listen to who was having an affair with whom; who was getting breast implants; whose hair is really mousy brown; and who was lying to their partner. Often, I found myself being fed right into the gossip and giving my take on things. I was also in charge of personnel company-wide by that time, so I handled all of the staff's complaints and issues. And there were still the customers to deal with, of course.

I found myself slipping away, back into sadness, because of the endless stream of petty complaints. Not only that, but I wanted more out of life than just a paycheck and material possessions. Society seems to bombard us with the idea that having "stuff" will make us feel complete, but alas, it didn't make me happy.

I was feeling cheated by society.

By then I was renting a house with John, who was working in Phoenix in a design showroom, and some nights I would be so flustered from dealing with unhappy clients that I'd only grunt hello. We would head to the swimming pool in the back-yard and I'd just float, for as long as it took me to relax. Daisy and John's dog, Rocco, would lay their heads on the side of the pool and watch as we drifted on the surface, sometimes for hours, looking up at the sky.

What was building inside of me was the knowledge that it was time, yet again, to move on. But I didn't know to what—or where. One day, while floating in the pool, I talked to John about what was going on inside me.

"Spencer," he replied calmly. "You have been at this cross-road in your life before. You have been sad and not known where to turn. What did you do last time to pull yourself up out of your funk?"

I thought back to the first time I was in the hospital alone after my surgeries.

I thought back to the first time I was bullied.

I thought back to not knowing anyone at first in middle school.

I thought back to the hardships in my first year of university.

"I surrendered," I said to him. "Yes!" I added, enthusiasti-cally. That was the next lesson I had to learn—or relearn, actu-ally. I had to let go. I had learned back in first year of college how to be alone. Now I was being asked to find my true path, to be authentic to my vision and myself. I had to let whatever forces wanted to move me, move me. I had to continue on in my journey.

Not long after that, Reed called. He asked me if I wanted to go to Kenya.

Chapter 10

*As soon as I got my passport back from the Kenyan cus-
toms officer at Jomo Kenyatta International Airport in
Nairobi, I wheeled over to Reed.* I was still thinking about
that voice I had heard in my head—*But you're here for something else ... you will find the answer. Africa has a way of calling people back to themselves*—and at first I didn't hear Reed
speaking to me.

"Are you listening?" he said, looking at me quizzically.
"We're finally here!"

I shook my head and then nodded. "Sorry, I was just lost
in thought," I said, as we made our way to the baggage
pick-up area.

"Kenya! What a flight. London was a riot," Reed continued.
He was referring to our adventure during our layover in London's Heathrow Airport. Gate agents tend to fuss when I'm

getting on airplanes, so Reed and I were offered rides on those golf carts with no roofs, the ones that almost run you down in the airport and are usually either completely empty or full of purple-haired grandmothers and balding grandfathers. Reed turned to me and said: "Ha, our very own personal escort. Let's take advantage of this and pretend I'm famous."

We had an hour's layover in London. A large woman with dyed blonde hair offered to drive us around in her cart. "You might get lost," she said to Reed. "I think it would be best if I drove you, so nothing happens to your friend here." Reed sat on the back and waved to the people we passed. Many waved back because Reed, despite his sweatpants, looked like a movie star, with his salt and pepper hair, dark tan, white teeth and dark sunglasses. I began yelling out to people that he was the mayor of Miami. Reed also has this incredible way of making me feel comfortable, which makes me sometimes do things I wouldn't normally do. This example is a case in point.

And eight hours later we were in Kenya. When we reached the baggage area, Reed wandered off to hug his partner, Greg, and Greg's sister, Alawna. We were all part of the group sent by Free The Children to help build two schools. Reed had raised the money in North America for all of the supplies.

As I waited by myself for the baggage to drop down into the carousel, I thought back to my experiences at the customs desk, when the customs officer looked at me so intently. And once again, I heard a voice in the back of my head: *You're here for something else, too. You will find the answer. Africa has a way of calling people back to themselves.*

I just wish I knew, I thought to myself. *Why I am* really *here.*

The next two days were so busy I had little time to think about the answer to that question. Although at our hotel in Nairobi, the first order of business was sleep, which came the moment my head hit the pillow.

The next morning started with an upset stomach after discovering too late that my usual breakfast of Corn Flakes does not sit well served with hot milk. My queasiness worsened as I made my way with Greg's family through the congested streets of Nairobi in the back of a Land Rover, bouncing around in the back seat. Motorbikes kicked up black smoke as they weaved in and out of traffic. Men on bicycles raised their fists in protest at the taxis that swerved too close to them. Everywhere I looked, women in red, yellow, blue, white and orange Kenyan outfits carried wicker baskets on their heads and bundles of wood on their backs.

Our destination was an elephant sanctuary on the outskirts of Nairobi. But what in my quiet hometown of Rock Springs would have involved a half-hour drive, along smoothly paved roads, took about two hours in Kenya. Kenyan roads are full of potholes and they are very dusty. By the time we entered the sanctuary and I got out of the SUV, I was gasping for air and holding my stomach from the cramps. I was overwhelmed not only by the warm milk, but also the sights, smells and diversity of the Kenyan culture. It was sensory overload. I wanted to turn around and go back. Home! *What am I doing in Africa?* I asked myself.

Then I looked up. I found myself staring into the dopey eyes of a baby elephant with long eyelashes. She had a look on her face as if to say: *Who are you?*

For almost all of my childhood, I had a stuffed elephant—it was grey, soft and about the size of a newborn baby. I called it Dumbo. I slept with that elephant. I took Dumbo to the grocery store with Mom and to our cabin in the woods of Pinedale, Wyoming. I taught Dumbo how to swim, how to fish and how to ride a skateboard. During the most painful periods of my childhood, when I had to spend nights alone at the hospital, Dumbo was right there beside me.

When red stuffing began falling from his seams, my mother would sew him up. Eventually Dumbo became so tattered that his cuddly fur was replaced by coarse hair and multicolored thread. Finally, an ear fell off. Nonetheless, Dumbo was my best friend. All through high school, even, he sat perched on my bookshelf, looking down at me as I completed my algebra and English homework.

On my second day in Kenya I found myself looking into the eyes of a real-life Dumbo. All of my aches and pains vanished. I reached out a hand to touch one of the creature's ears. It shook its head, spun around and shuffled off, the red and blue blanket it was wearing billowing out at the sides.

The sanctuary is an orphanage for elephants and rhinoceroses. It was founded by David Sheldrick and his wife Daphne and is located in the park the couple also created—Tsavo East National Park. One of the goals of the sanctuary is to care for orphaned baby elephants for the entire period they would normally stay with their mothers, before reintroducing them to the wild. Even then, most of the animals don't wander out of Tsavo Park.

The little elephant friend who greeted me and reminded me so much of Dumbo soon became lost among a herd of its peers, many of which were also wearing blankets on their backs. I was told that many babies die from pneumonia, especially during the cool nights of Kenya's rainy season, which we were in the midst of. By midday, thick grey clouds would cover the royal blue sky.

After visiting the elephants, we were scheduled to go to a giraffe sanctuary. Before we left, however, I sat for a moment by myself and stared off at a baby rhinoceros chewing on some grass by a tall acacia tree. Something stirred inside me—a knowing, as if the answer I had been seeking was about to arise.

The Giraffe Center at Langata was founded by Betty and Jack Leslie-Melville in 1979 as a sanctuary for the endangered Rothschild giraffe. One of the center's main features is an observation platform that looks like a big tree fort. I left my wheelchair at the bottom and climbed up. Once in the tree fort, I looked over a small fence at the giraffes. They would stretch their long necks up to stare at me. Satisfied that I was harmless, they would then open their mouths and I would feed them small pellets of food. I also had the option of putting one of the pellets between my lips and letting the giraffe lick my face and take it directly from my mouth. But after seeing the huge string of giraffe drool on Alawna, I decided against it.

And, being a gentleman, I never kiss on the first date.

Reed and Greg didn't join us on our visits that day. They were busy working on the documentary film they were making in Kenya. Reed was now working for WSVN in Miami, having left his job at the ABC affiliate in Salt Lake City. He had already begun raising money for Free The Children to build schools in Africa before he moved to Miami in 2007. Also in 2007, he traveled to Kenya to build his first school. He'd been scheduled to return in the spring of 2008 to complete another building. And it was just before the 2007 Christmas holidays, when I would soon be leaving Phoenix for a snowy Christmas in Wyoming, that Reed had called.

"I had a thought," he announced in his great broadcaster voice. "You should come to Kenya with us. I was thinking that Kenya might help you through your funk."

At first I said no.

I didn't have enough money to cover my airfare. I also would have to take extra time off work, and I was using most of my vacation time for my Christmas holidays. A few days later, however, I had a phone conversation with my aunt Jamie.

"Spencer," she said, after I told her about Reed's invitation, "I think this is an amazing opportunity and I would hate for you to pass it up. Don't let the money stop you. If you feel comfortable, I know Phillip and I and the rest of the family would be more than happy to help you raise the money to go." Jamie continued: "This is a once in a lifetime opportunity and it would be really nice if you could take advantage of it. With Reed backing you up and encouraging you, it's something you should seriously consider."

My aunt and uncle's generosity touched me, but I initially said no thanks. It was just too much to ask. But the more I thought about it, the more the idea of traveling to Kenya consumed me and the more I realized I had to go. Why? I wasn't sure. But something in my gut just felt right, so I humbly accepted the offer from my family.

The trip, once booked, nearly didn't happen, though. At the end of December, Kenya erupted in civil unrest when Mwai Kibaki was declared the winner of the presidential election. His main opponent, Raila Odinga, declared that the election was rigged and international observers confirmed something was askew. The people of Kenya took to the streets in protest. For nearly two weeks, the nightly news in the United States broadcasted reports of rallies and killings, including the slaughter of thirty people in a church in Eldoret, in the Great Rift Valley of Kenya, on New Year's Day.

Kenya, once a British colony, is a poor country in East Africa. In 2010, it was ranked at number 147 on the United Nations Human Development Index, out of 182 countries—meaning it lacks universal schooling for children and youth, basic health care that we take for granted in North America and access to jobs. It is best known in the West for its spectacular wildlife and terrain. The bestselling book *Out of Africa* by Karen Blixen, who wrote under the pen name Isak Dineson, is about Kenya and was made into a film. (Our Nairobi hotel, which was a series of cabins and a main lodge, was called the Karen Blixen Coffee Garden Restaurant and Cottages.)

Reed is a newsman, so when the U.S. Department of State at last issued a notice that it was safe for us to travel to Kenya to build the school, he decided to also film some of the post-electoral violence in Nairobi's slum areas, including Kibera, one of East Africa's largest slums. Reed and Greg would be gone from our group making their documentary film until a few days into our trek to the Maasai Mara.

That night, after my day spent at the sanctuaries, was a lonely one without Reed and Greg around. I had a cabin all to myself, in a foreign city I'd barely experienced yet. But my nerves eventually settled and in those moments when I was half asleep, half awake, my mind drifted to the face of that baby elephant. I remembered Dumbo. And I felt somewhat more at ease.

The eight-seat airplane we took the next morning to reach the Maasai Mara flew low over the Serengeti. I watched zebras and wildebeests scatter in all different directions, spooked by the sound of the airplane engine. My first and only other trip to Africa was when I was fifteen, when Grandpa West and my Dad took me hunting in South Africa. I've never shared their passion for hunting. The men in my family, who hunt elk, deer and the occasional moose, have a great deal of respect for the animals they kill. Starting when I was a small child, my Dad would bundle me up on a chilly, windy day to go look for antelope. But I've never shared their passion.

Seeing the wildlife below, out the plane window, gave me a thought: *Maybe I'm supposed to be a wildlife activist? May-*

be that's why I am here—I'm supposed to return to the Unit-ed States and fight for the rights of animals! I smiled at the thought. My family would of course support any decision I made. *Maybe*, I thought. *Maybe.*

My mind then churned out other possibilities. My under-graduate degree had been in communications. So maybe I was meant to make the film with Reed. But then, Reed didn't want me joining him, and for good reason. They brought enough attention to themselves in the poor slums of Kibera with their white skin and cameras. I would have been a major distrac-tion. Maybe, then, I was meant to abandon my American life to work at the elephant sanctuary. A good friend once told me that in shamanism, the elephant represents luck, wisdom and good fortune. An elephant was the totem animal of the Indian god Shiva the Destroyer, who sought to banish illusion from the mind and encourage clarity. And Buddhists believe that the Buddha shows himself in the form of a white elephant.

I was still thinking of all the possible reasons why I was in Kenya when our airplane landed on a dirt airstrip. When I got out of the plane there were rolling hills, long savannah grasses and majestic acacia trees as far as I could see in all directions.

Robin Wiszowaty, an American from the Chicago area who has lived in Kenya for many years, was there to meet us when we got off the plane. The others began walking to the Free The Children headquarters, a few kilometers away, while Robin whisked me into a white Land Rover. En route, she ex-plained to me that Free The Children not only builds schools but implements clean water projects and health and sanitation programs. They also help the Maasai people, including women, develop and manage their own small businesses. Free The Children provides education for children, and for adults looking for alternative ways to earn money.

"Let me teach you some phrases in Swahili that you should know when you meet the Maasai," Robin said.

Habari yako? "How are you?"

Asante sana. "Thank you very much."

Jambo rafiki. "Hello, friend."

I rolled the phrases over my tongue for the rest of the day and well into the evening as we sat around the stone fireplace on big cream-colored cushions.

"Tomorrow," Robin ended the night saying. "You can start using these phrases when we head out to the villages, to see the schools we've already built, and the place where we're going to build the new school."

The next day, the Land Rover bumped down a small hill and then up again into the village of Emori Joi. Along the road were children of all ages, who, upon hearing the vehicle, dropped everything they were doing and came running toward us to wave and yell *"Jambo."* The scenery was breathtaking. A valley full of acacia trees, cornfields and beautiful yet simple homes made from mud, cow dung and sticks. And instead of using wood, steel or vinyl to fence off their properties, the villagers used cacti.

Even though my watch said it was only ten a.m., the sun was hot and high in the sky. I hadn't slept well the night before. Bush babies, the small animals that Robin had warned me about, would cry long into the night, keeping me awake for hours, even after the generator was turned off and I was left in complete darkness. I just lay on my bed listening to the eerie calls of the bush babies and the wind rustling the leaves of the trees until the natural light of the sun came dancing into my room in the early hours of the morning.

As we neared our destination, our SUV turned off the main dirt road onto a smaller one, visible only by its deep wheel tracks. Trees and bushes, many with thorns the size of tiger claws, slapped at the sides of the vehicle until we bumped our way over potholes into the middle of a clearing. Our driver drove right up into a football field-sized area surrounded by five cement buildings the size of tennis courts.

As soon as I exited the car, I was swarmed by children—children wearing royal blue school uniforms with skirts and slacks and beige cotton button-down shirts. Children with short-cropped hair; children with big white toothy smiles. A small boy reached out to touch me, then withdrew his hand quickly.

"Jambo, rafiki. Jambo, rafiki. Jambo, rafiki," I said, they said, we all said over and over again.

One of the older girls moved toward me and waved for her friends to stand back. She then gestured for me to follow her, which I did, moving across the clearing in my wheelchair as she skipped her way to one of the buildings.

Inside, the building was dark. The only light in the single cavernous room was that which came in through four tiny windows. The girl handed me a workbook and kept pointing at it, to indicate it was hers. I opened up the front cover and saw line after line of English. This young girl started to point to English words in her book and motioned for me to read them to her. We spent the rest of our time together pointing out words and saying them to each other.

Then I heard laughter coming from outside. The girl peered out one of the windows and waved for me to come. All of the children who had greeted me, and many more, had congregated outside the building and were jumping up and down. Robin, who was with them, explained: "The children want to ask you some questions. Can they? I will translate."

"Of course," I said. For exactly the reason Reed worried about taking me to Kibera, the children of Emori Joi found me a fascination. I walked out of the schoolroom on my hands and met the kids, the younger ones being about the same height as me. I pulled myself back into my wheelchair, which I had parked outside.

"Where are you from?" a tall girl, maybe about age thirteen, asked first.

"I am from the United States," I replied.

"Ahhh," the crowd hummed.

"How did you get here?" a young boy with a gap between his two front teeth then asked.

"On an airplane," I said, pointing to the sky and then flapping my hands like a bird. The younger children in the group giggled.

"Are you religious?" a child of about eight asked me. I had to think about the answer. "Hmm. *I am spiritual,*" I eventually replied. "But I don't go to any particular church to worship.

Spirituality is in here," I said, cupping my hands and placing them over my heart.

Three very young children stepped forward and gently ran their fingers over my chest.

"Are you a doctor?" another child asked.

I laughed. "No, my uncle is a doctor, but—" I stopped, not quite knowing what to say. "I... I... I have another path that I am following," I eventually replied, thinking as I said this, *I just wish I knew where to find that path.*

"Is it hard to get around in your wheelchair?" a girl asked.

I smiled. This is usually the first question children ask me. "No," I replied. I had Robin ask the children to step back. I then moved the wheelchair toward the girl. When I was in front of her, I popped a wheelie and spun the chair and myself around in circles like a spinning top.

"Ooooh!" the children purred.

When the crowd had settled down, the same girl raised her hand to speak. "You know," she said. *"Sikujua hiyo kitu inge-fanyika wazungu pia."*

My eyes grew wide as Robin translated the girl's words for me: "I didn't know that things like this happened to white people."

Robin leaned forward and spoke to me in a hushed voice. "Spencer, you've taught the children a valuable lesson today. It doesn't matter where we come from or what color our skin is, we all have obstacles we have to face in life, whether you come from North America or Africa."

I could feel tears beginning to well in the corners of my eyes.

"See that man over there?" Robin continued, pointing to

a tall, heavy man standing by the school construction site and looking out over the savannah. "His name is Paul and he pulled me aside while you were in the school. He said he feels you are very special—special for coming here. You are a shining example that anything is possible and if someone like you with no legs can travel all this way to help build a school, almost anything is possible."

I stared at the young girl who had spoken. *"Asante sana,"* I mouthed.

"OK," Robin then said, clapping her hands. "The children want to sing for you."

The group broke into a song in Swahili, and Robin translated:

We are playing in a field, and we are touching our heads.

We are playing in a field, and we are dancing.

The children then swung their hips from side to side, while twirling around in a circle.

We are playing in a field, making music.

The children pretended to play guitars.

I clapped and danced in my wheelchair along with them. When the song finished, the children prodded me to sing a Western song. I mulled over the pieces I knew well enough and decided on the song I always listen to when I am feeling sad and blue: Barbara Streisand's "A Piece of Sky."

When I was finished, Robin translated a few of the lines for the children:

Tell me where

Where is it written?

What it is I'm meant to be?

That I can't dare.

I didn't have much time, at first, to reflect on my visit with the schoolchildren. I was immediately whisked away by Reed to help with the building of the schools. In one of the two buildings, the foundation had been dug and half a wall had been constructed, perhaps by some of the Maasai villagers or a Free The Children group who had come before us. I helped lay the mortar and smoothed it out with a trowel. I did one row and then another. I got dirty and sweaty and loved every minute of the four days I worked on the school. It gave me a great sense of accomplishment to work on this new school.

Towards the end of our trip, our Maasai guides Nabala and Wilson took us on a walk of the community where we were asked to help some of the girls and the mamas of the community carry water back to their house. The hill was quite steep so Nabala wrapped me in a red and blue *shukah* and tossed me on his back and took me for a walk down to the Maasai River, helping me practise my new words in Swahili.

Later that night, as we ate dinner by the fire, Robin told me about foreman Paul, who had seen me and approached her at the school in the afternoon. He said he felt humbled and that it takes great courage and spirit to travel all this way in my condition and that he wanted to shake my hand. But he didn't because all the kids were following me, but maybe he would have the courage tomorrow. Robin also shared with me that the superintendent was equally impressed. He told her and the students at the assembly earlier that day how lucky they were to have such an incredible teacher. I was overwhelmed and I didn't know how to show my thanks and appreciation.

That evening, I sat out on the stone patio of the Free The Children center under a beautiful blanket of stars. I thought about Reed and all of our conversations about me being a public speaker. I thought about that customs officer. I thought about that little girl in Emori Joi, who had said she didn't know things like this happened to white people. I thought about my loving family, who never made me feel like I was handicapped. I thought about my stuffed animal, Dumbo, and the baby elephant at the sanctuary.

Why are you really here? I whispered to myself.

And then it hit me. It hit me just like that warm Kenyan air for the first time when we landed.

Reed is right. I can inspire people to do whatever they want and to love who they are despite what they look like, where they were born and who they were born to. In the end, aren't we all unique and special? I just happen to wear my differences on the outside, because I have no legs. I could use my story to help students realize that we can all lend a helping hand. But as a speaker, (yes, Reed wins this round) it was now my responsibility to "pass the torch" to others. To help them recognize the power they have to make a difference. It was also a way to highlight the incredible people doing amazing things around the world as well as paying homage to the mentors who had helped me see this as well.

That was it—I now *needed* to be a mentor for others.

When I returned from Kenya in the spring of 2008, I knew my time in Phoenix was nearing an end. I couldn't stay on at Dolce after all that I had seen in Africa. I felt it would be an injustice to what I had learned about the country, about poverty, about Africa and about me.

Despite the fact that my life was in transition yet again, I wasn't depressed. I actually felt a joyfulness, a trust even, that I was being taken care of. "I am being guided somewhere," I said to Reed at one point. I knew where I was heading with my journey.

Before I slipped into sleep at night, I'd hear that young girl in Kenya who said: *"Sikujua hiyo kitu ingefanyika wazungu pia."*

I didn't know that things like this happened to white people.

One day, I was driving down the street and slipped on Jason Mraz's "Details in the Fabric" on my stereo. I sang along: "Hold your own, know your name and go your own way."

At the end, I whispered: *"Asante sana"*—"thank you" in Swahili.

Robin, in Kenya, and I, in North America, were now e-mailing quite regularly. I was also perusing the Free The Children website, wondering about—dreaming of—working for them, but not thinking it possible. Finally, I saw a job opening on the website. They were looking for a tour speaker who could visit schools and universities and talk about, among other things, the United Nations Millennium Development Goals. Some 192 countries had agreed to achieve eight worldwide goals by 2015, including reducing extreme poverty, improving child mortality rates and fighting disease epidemics such as HIV/AIDS.

"Why not apply?" Robin encouraged me in an e-mail. "You have nothing to lose."

I polished off my résumé and Robin sent Free The Children a reference letter about the time she had spent with me in Kenya. I then started to write a short letter describing myself. What Kenya had shown me most was what Reed had known a few years earlier; I discovered the power of my own story and how it could bridge divides. While I viewed myself as just another kid, now a young man, the outside world saw my efforts to fit in and lead a normal life as truly remarkable and uplifting. What I had learned was that we all *do* suffer in our own ways. We all have our own journeys to walk or, in my case, wheel through. And when we celebrate together the obstacles we have surmounted, we come together, and that is the beginning of community.

After my letter was done, I sent my application in electronically. A few days later, a representative from Free The Children called and asked if I could come to Toronto, Canada, for an interview. I was ecstatic.

A day after my interview and a presentation showcasing my public speaking abilities, I was given the news: I had the job.

I returned to Arizona, submitted my resignation letter and began packing. I would spend a few weeks in Rock Springs, before moving to Canada and begin my new life as a public speaker.

On a clear, balmy July night in Rock Springs, Mom hosted a barbecue to say goodbye. The next day I was leaving not just Wyoming, but the United States. My cousins Mitchell and Emily, Aunt Jamie and Uncle Phillip and my parents and grandparents were all there—and Daisy, of course, who I was leaving with Mom. I would be too busy in Canada to give Daisy the life she deserved. It was tough to say goodbye to Daisy, just like it had been with Zac, but it was for the better. Part of my job with Free The Children involved traveling across Canada and the United States for speeches, so I wouldn't be home. I also could be going to countries like India and Kenya, talking with students and introducing them to Free The Children programs.

Mom and Aunt Jamie were in the kitchen tossing green salads and putting the garnish on potato and macaroni salads. Grandma Callas was arranging the dessert tray of homemade chocolate brownies and potica cookies. And Grandpa Callas was passing around the beer and wine.

I made my way outside to join my cousins and sister, who were sitting back on some lounge chairs. I plopped myself down beside Mitchell and looked over at Uncle Phillip and Dad, who were barbecuing spare ribs and steaks. Dad was recounting yet another hunting story.

"One time I was off in the bush with my cousin. I was hiding underneath some leaves, when I heard the sounds of branches breaking on top of me—"

While I had been listening to this particular story since I was a baby, I still smiled. I loved my Dad. I loved his hunting stories. I wouldn't be where I am today had he been any different.

"My favorite band of all time is Metallica," I then caught Mitchell telling Annie.

I turned to Mitchell. He was thirteen years younger than me, well over six feet tall, a star high school football player and a whiz in school, particularly in languages and mathematics. As he continued talking about Metallica, I remembered him, way back when he was about two. I used to climb his Dad, Uncle Phillip, like he was a jungle gym. When Mitchell was a toddler, he used to climb me in much the same way. Once, when I was giving him a bubble bath, he stopped to stare at me. I was perched on the toilet, making sure he washed his hair in between playing with his toy cars.

"Benz," Mitchell said that day. He couldn't pronounce "s" properly yet and Benz was the name he had somehow slipped into using when talking to me. "Benz," he continued. "You don't have any legs!"

"No, Mitchell," I replied. "I don't."

"OK!" He then went back to what he was doing.

Nearly fourteen years later, that little boy was grown up. "One of my dreams," he continued, "is that I am at a Metallica concert. They announce that the bass player is sick and ask if there is anyone in the audience who can replace him. I raise my hand and Metallica invites me up on stage. I do so well, I become a permanent member of the band!"

Emily came out of the guest bedroom dressed in a pale yellow formal dress that was once her mother's prom dress. She twirled around, like a model, for us to see. "I dreamt about *Harry Potter* last night," she said, her soft brown hair framing her face. "You know the spider? In my dream Grandpa's cat came in and turned into the spider. I was very scared and then I woke up."

"You look beautiful, Emily," I said, admiring her dress. I could just see Aunt Jamie in that dress, going to prom with Uncle Phillip, holding his hand and declaring at age sixteen that they would be together forever. Emily was trying the dress on as a potential costume. She was performing in the ensemble for a musical staging of *Grease*.

"I have a dream, too," Annie spoke up. "Don't forget about me."

"What is your dream?" Mitchell probed.

"I want to be a nurse one day. I want to help people."

I smiled. Annie made me so proud. Most of her life, she had to deal with living in my shadow. "Oh, you're Spencer's sister, the guy with no legs," kids would say to her. Their parents or older people in the community would always ask about Annie after me first.

"How is Spencer?" they would ask. And almost as an afterthought, add, "How are you, Annie?" Despite this, she had grown into a caring, beautiful young woman, with eyes like our mother's. She had also left Phoenix, and had taken on a job making sure home-care patients in Rock Springs had their oxygen tanks. She was on-call twenty-four hours a day and never complained. She would sometimes spend hours with just one customer if there weren't others lining up for her help, talking to him or her about their needs and what she could do to offer assistance.

"Spence," Emily chimed in. "Tell us one of your dreams."

"I... I..." I couldn't think of what to say, other than I hoped to see them all again very soon. I didn't have any scary or hopeful dream to recount just then.

After dinner, Mom and I found ourselves alone on the porch.

"So how do you feel about moving to Toronto?" she asked.

"I think I am really going to miss Daisy," I said. "My heart hurts already with the thought of saying goodbye to her."

"Now you know how I feel every time you and Annie leave," she said, with a weak smile. "But you have to follow your heart, and that makes me happy."

"I'll miss you, Mom," I replied.

"I'll miss you, too," she said. "Here," she added, holding up a copy of *The Alchemist*. "I bought this for you. Let me read you something: 'Before a dream is realized, the Soul of the World tests everything that was learned along the way.'"

Chapter 11

Since I became a speaker for Free The Children in August 2008, my schedule has been non-stop. During the school year, I give talks every day during the week, sometimes even two times a day and on weekends, to high school and elementary school kids. I tell the assemblies my life story in hopes of inspiring them, to let them know that they can overcome whatever obstacles they have in their lives and that they, too, can make a difference in this world. And I believe every word—because it worked for me.

"It doesn't matter what color your skin is, where you come from or what your gender or sexual orientation is," I often say in my speeches. "We all have the ability and the responsibility to lend a helping hand to someone who needs it."

I also quote Martin Luther King, Jr.: "If you want to be important—wonderful. If you want to be recognized—wonderful. If you want to be great—wonderful. But recognize that he who is the greatest among you shall be your servant. That's a new definition of greatness."

"You must stop looking at the world through your head. You must look through your heart instead," I also say, reciting Elizabeth Gilbert's line from the blockbuster book *Eat, Pray, Love*.

My new job—which is a lifestyle, more than a job—also involves my taking part in We Day events. These are held in cities across North America, arenas stuffed to capacity with youth passionate about social change. Our audiences for We Day sometimes number in the tens of thousands. At these events, I share the stage with music stars and social-political leaders. Once, I spoke alongside Nobel Peace Prize laureates His Holiness the Dalai Lama and Elie Wiesel. Jason Mraz was there too, whose music inspired me to be strong enough to go against the norm and follow my own path. His lyrics have always stuck with me. The Dalai Lama imparted to me the words to describe what I feel instinctively, but could not articulate on my own. He said, for instance, that what is missing in the world today is compassion and we are raising a generation of indifferent bystanders. I partly agree with him. But I believe that the generations that have come before mine have laid the foundation for this. Nonetheless, if you are reading this book, chances are you are among the large and growing number of young people in the world today who are not just demanding change, but living it.

My most special moments with Free The Children, however, are those I have spent out in the field. Getting to meet the children who have benefited most from the growing numbers of young people who are making the change from "me" thinking to "we" thinking. I felt this most profoundly in July 2010, when my plane landed in Udaipur, India.

It was my first time to the second most populated country on earth. My mind played tricks on me before I left, telling me I was sure to get sick from the food. (I have a very sensitive stomach and can't eat a lot of spices. Anyone I knew who had been to India chimed in with his or her advice—just eat the rice. No, just eat the fruit. No, just the vegetables. In the end, I was absolutely fine.)

But my senses were in overdrive. Immediately I was hit with the poverty of the country. The streets of Udaipur were packed with rickshaws and cows, people and motorbikes ... and garbage. Poverty was right in my face, from rundown shantytown homes to homeless youth begging in the streets. As our Land Rover slowly snaked through the congested city streets, I stopped and stared at one point at a young boy, possibly age six, lugging big blocks of ice as men stood around him and gawked. One of the men seemed to be the store owner and shouted orders at the child. The child was dirty and wearing torn and tattered clothes. The store owner was clad in what appeared to be an expensive cotton shirt and dress pants. He was tall and his hair was dyed orange, and he just stood there drinking a cup of steaming chai tea.

As I watched this scene, I thought of Craig Kielburger, who co-founded Free The Children with his brother, Marc. In 1995, Craig read a story in the newspaper about a twelve-year-old boy who had been murdered in Pakistan. That child, Iqbal Masih, had been forced into bonded labor in a carpet factory when he was four. Craig, himself only twelve, started to read and study the human rights violations against children around the world. He was angered by what he was reading and founded Free The Children with some classmates. He even traveled to South Asia and saw the plight of some of the children first hand. Believing that education is the best way to fight child labor, Craig established a system that linked schools in North America and Europe with schools in developing countries. Over the years, Craig and his group collected and distributed school and health supplies to over 100,000 schools. Then they started building schools in poor, rural areas.

Sadly, the Iqbals of the world still exist. This is one of the reasons why Marc and Craig founded Free The Children and developed the concept for We Day: to empower young people everywhere to make a difference. Every child, after all, has the right to an education, to a name, to have a home and food and to be loved. And those of us in the West need to do what we can to make sure our sisters and brothers in this world have the same.

Back in Udaipur, our Land Rover eventually reached the outskirts of the city and made its way over the bumpy rural roads to a small village called Lai. I would be spending the next three weeks in Lai, leading a group of twenty or so high school students as they dug the foundation for a new school. The mostly Canadian students were scheduled to arrive in two days. I was the sentinel: sent early to make sure their sleeping quarters were ready and that the supplies to build the foundation had arrived.

When the students showed up, my job was to supervise them, lead them through this experience, instill leadership skills and answer their questions about Free The Children. Among the many charitable projects Free The Children runs is Adopt a Village. Schools and youth groups across the world choose a country where Free The Children works, and then raises funds to help a village with its education, health care, clean water and income needs. For instance, Free The Children has started income-generating programs for women in Kenya, so that the women can help support their children.

In Lai, however, we were focusing on the education needs of a goat-herding community. Before Free The Children built their first school in Lai in 1996, the children didn't go to school. They would spend their days goat herding and would marry at very young ages. But because so many children wanted, and needed, an education more schools had to be built.

Lai has been hit hard by years of drought. Sadly, this has had an impact on the families' already low incomes. The children's school uniforms were dirty and torn. Every second child was barefoot—and those who had shoes wore dirty, and sometimes broken, flip-flops.

While our group mixed cement, used pickaxes to cut the rocks and removed huge boulders, the children of Lai would surround us. They would skip out of the one-room school-house that already had been built by Free The Children before heading home for dinner, sing to us and tell us about their lives, what they were studying at school and what they wanted to be when they were older. There were future teachers, doctors, nurses, engineers and even a scientist among them. School, some of the children told me via a translator, meant a chance for them to create better lives for themselves and for their families. I knew it meant they didn't have to go to work at age five.

Some of the children explained that adults were often drinking the local alcoholic brew to excess. They didn't want to follow in the footsteps of the adults who got drunk all the time. These children created an "awareness day" to tell other students and any adult who attended the risks associated with prolonged alcohol use. It was amazing how driven they were to succeed, despite all of the obstacles in their way.

Except for the dirty school uniforms and girls' gold earrings and bangles, the children looked like school kids anywhere in the world. Their faces were bright and their smiles beamed. They wanted to learn. Seeing and feeling their eagerness forced me to look back at the times I was in school and took studying for granted. I had opportunities that these children couldn't even fathom. But I knew one thing for certain: any one of these children would have excelled in that computer science course I failed. They would have given it their all. Unlike me.

On one of our days off from building the school, the North American students and I visited one of the orphanages that Mother Teresa established in Udaipur. The tiny nuns who greeted us at the front door, some no older than me, were Mother Teresa look-alikes—they wore the white dress and white habit with royal blue stripes, just like the Nobel Peace Prize winner had.

The children, however, were visibly ill. One had Down's syndrome; another laid on the floor the entire time, rocking back and forth. I learned that some of the children were orphans; others had families that were too poor to care for them, due to the children's various health needs. I didn't speak for a long time after the visit to the orphanage. I kept thinking about the children: they had no one, except the nuns. My melancholy began to lift as I thought about those nuns. All of them had families they had willingly left behind to dedicate their lives to these children. The children, while sick, were all happy, clean and well fed. It reminded me of something Mother Teresa once said: "We cannot do great things on this earth. Only small things with great love."

The nuns were an example of this. They received very little recognition for their hard work. They lived in poverty, except for the donations Westerners sent them to keep the orphanage open. Despite these challenges, however, the nuns exuded love: love for the children, love for humanity.

I realized then that the turning point for me was my first trip to Kenya, which sparked in me the need to dedicate my entire life to being in service to others, too. This was the missing part of my being. Up until then—going to school, pursuing my acting and then working in the beauty industry—I had led a typical North American middle-class life. My room was full of "things." My head was full of selfish wants and dreams. But nothing fulfilled me. I was lacking the most basic need of all: giving back. My new life with Free The Children was all about giving back and I felt rewarded. I may not be able to help Mother Teresa's orphans directly, but I was helping the children in the village of Lai, including an eight-year-old named Leila, by providing them with a proper school.

When Leila first showed up at the one-room schoolhouse, which had one teacher instructing about a hundred students, the other children laughed at her. She was small for her age and dirty. She smelled, for she hadn't taken a bath, perhaps in weeks. Leila was the brunt of jokes and sneers for months. But she persevered because she wanted to go to school and make something of herself. She eventually learned to bathe properly and was given a brand-new crisp school uniform that she kept clean. Leila tuned out the ridicule and focused on becoming the best student and helper she could be. I learned that she also showed up early at the classroom in the mornings and would sweep the stairs before her peers arrived. She even came out and assisted us in laying the foundation for the new schoolhouse. She reminded me of something else Mother Teresa once said: "Do not wait for leaders; do it alone, person-to-person."

When Leila wasn't helping us build the school, or in school herself, she would sit on a small mound not far from us, and with her chin cupped in her hands, watch us build. It was very difficult for me to say goodbye to Leila when I had to leave India. She reminded me of me—an outcast. But one who was doing her part, nonetheless. There was a connection that I just couldn't put into words.

After Lai, I was on a plane heading to Nairobi. It was to be my third trip to Kenya. Despite being tired from my time in India, I could not sleep a wink the night before we departed. Whenever I thought about Kenya, I felt a calmness flow through me. After all, Kenya brought me home to myself. The soft winds and acacia trees sang a song to me. I was able to look inward.

Every time I arrived in Nairobi, I searched the faces of the customs officers, looking for the one I had first met, who'd asked me my name. If I had seen him, I would have thanked him, even though I suppose he would have thought me crazy. Alas, he was never there when I was there. Perhaps he was just a figment of my imagination, the Fool card in the tarot deck who initiates my journey—or the hero's journey within, as Gigi Jasper would say.

The Nairobi streets of July 2010 were much the way I remembered: congested with people, bicycles, cars with their horns blaring, women carrying baskets of fruit and vegetables on their heads for the market, men and women in polished business suits. But there was also something different about Nairobi, an energy in the air I had not felt before. I soon learned why. All of Kenya was voting in a national referendum in August. They were voting for a new constitution, to replace the existing constitution that was drafted when the country was still under colonial rule. They were voting for a new constitution that enshrined human rights for all, a judiciary that would be separate from the political system and laws that would protect women and children from abuse and outdated traditional practices like the genital mutilation of girls.

Foreigners working in Nairobi were worried. They were tense, fearing that the referendum would end with the same results as the 2007 presidential election: civil war. The country was still rebuilding from that one, the aftermath of which Reed had filmed when we first visited the country two years earlier.

I shook off the foreigners' worries. Nairobi felt vibrant to me, on the brink of something new and extraordinary—not war.

I spent two days in Nairobi, and made another visit to the giraffe sanctuary. Finally I got up the courage to allow the tall, elegant Rothschild giraffe to kiss me: a big, rough, slobbering kiss that made me really wonder what all the fuss was about. (I guess, technically, this means that I *do* kiss on the second date.)

After Nairobi, I headed to the Maasai Mara, which was once again my true destination. I was taking twenty-eight high school students to Sikirar, a community where Free The Children was building a new school. When completed, Sikirar would have three schoolhouses, as we had already completed two, so students could attend classes with no more than thirty other students at a time. Before the schools had been built, the children either didn't go to school or learned their lessons from teachers while sitting under a tree.

I was sad because I would not be visiting the Maasai community I had first visited back in 2008. I wanted to see that young girl again, who had said to me: "I didn't know that things like this happened to white people."

But I knew I would meet new children, who would have just as much of an impact on me as I hoped to have on their lives. Sikirar is a village located in the middle of a hayfield. When we arrived we saw swaying fields parched from the dry season that was well underway, and there were few acacia trees. As a result, the ground was really dusty and I could also see for miles and miles, all the way to rolling hills in the distance.

The people in Sikirar dressed elegantly. The women wore vibrant traditional Kenyan garb and the men wore colorful blankets over their shoulders. Both men and women were adorned with beaded headdresses. And the children, even the girls, had shaven heads, and wore green and white school uniforms.

My job, and that of the North American students, was not only to lay the foundation for the new school, but also to put up the walls. The villagers were to add the roof, making sure that the green tin they used would withstand the torrential downpours of the rainy season.

Almost from day one, a young boy named James and his friend Amos befriended me. Both children were perhaps eight and were the only two brave enough to walk forward and introduce themselves, before I had a chance to introduce myself to all of the children. These two boys became my entourage for the three weeks I was in Sikirar. They would take turns pushing me in my wheelchair, while the other sat on my lap, and we would race down the roads. We sang songs together and I taught them a few words in English. Occasionally, we even jumped rope. James and Amos were quite impressed with my gymnastic abilities!

A few times, I found myself alone with James, and we would sit quietly and look out over the hayfields. That was when James would teach me more Swahili words and sentences, like *Jino lako ni nani?* which is "What is your name?" I used them as often as I could.

Near the end of my three weeks in Sikirar, another non-profit group arrived at the compound where the two existing schools stood. They were handing out uniforms to some of the orphans in the community. I choked when I heard why they were there—the thought hadn't even crossed my mind that the children were orphans. All of the children acted like they belonged somewhere. I was told then that in the Maasai Mara, children who don't have parents have lots of aunties and uncles who will care for them. No child goes neglected, one of the village elders told me. "We all help to raise our young." I never asked why there was such a high rate of orphans in the Maasai Mara. But I can only speculate that one of the causes might be due to HIV/AIDS, which has felled so many Kenyans. In the Maasai Mara, it is still taboo to speak of the virus. Many people at funerals will not refer to the person as having died from AIDS-related illnesses, but of something else.

I learned that James, my bright-eyed friend, was also one of the orphans. The next time we found ourselves alone, I wanted to ask him about his family. But I couldn't get the words out.

A few days later, one of the mamas—the women at the school who cooked meals for the children—pulled me aside and said through a translator that she wanted to make me a beaded Maasai bracelet. I felt so honored.

"*Jino lako ni nani?*" she asked.

"Spencer," I replied.

"Pencer..." she repeated. "What does that mean?"

I laughed. In India and in Kenya no one could pronounce the "Sp" in Spencer, so I often ended up telling people to just call me Benson.

"Bensooon," the mama said, in her thick accent. "Do you have a Maasai name?"

Back in 2008, I was, in fact, given a Maasai name. Wilson, a Maasai warrior, had chosen it for me. Wilson, who works for Free The Children, had been my guide. Among his many duties, he teaches foreigners about Maasai culture and language. Wilson had touched my hands one evening as we were saying goodbye and said the next day he would return with my Maasai name. Sure enough he did. He explained that he had talked with several of the other Maasai warriors and they had decided that *Olopiro* was the perfect name for me.

"Olopiro," Wilson explained, "is the Swahili word for the wind that lifts up a bird."

"Olopiro is my Maasai name," I told the mama, a short, round woman with an even rounder face and a full smile. She giggled and then shook her head.

"I should have known," she said. "What a perfect name for you!"

On my very last day in Sikirar, the mama handed me a one-inch-thick beaded bracelet. It was orange and white, with a diagram of the Kenyan flag. On it was the word "Olo," for Olopiro.

Before heading back to Canada, I spent four days in Nairobi. I was there the morning after Kenya voted yes to their new constitution. There was no violence. I sat with some of the other Kenya facilitators and a sense of calm filled the house. The people had been given their country back. They would now have laws to support their progress.

In the late hours of my last night in Kenya, with a full moon hanging overhead, I found myself laying in bed, running my fingers over my new bracelet.

Olopiro, the wind that lifts up a bird. "What a fitting name," I said out loud. Not to mention my wingspan is huge. Wilson didn't choose it as my Maasai name because he felt I, alone, was the wind lifting up others. In Maasai culture, children are named in a ceremony, usually at the age of five. An elder in the community is called in and he comes up with the name. Sometimes, a child is named after the spirit or energies of their families or family members.

Not just in Maasai culture, but in many traditional societies around the world, great care is given to the naming of individuals—elders are sometimes called in, and even seers, who can look into the future and envision the life path of the person to be named.

Throughout my life, I have had many winds beneath my wings: starting with my mother, who fought for my best interests right from the beginning. My father and grandparents who gave me everything I needed to thrive; not always what

I wanted, but the tools to survive. My sister, who made me laugh. My friends, who made me realize it doesn't matter where you are from, but *who* you are inside.

I also had the wind of great teachers, like Reed Cowan and Ms. Jasper. And, of course, I now had Free The Children.

And my path for the future? I knew it involved working with, and for, others, particularly young adults and children. As an inspiration, or a gentle wind under their wings, so they could change their worlds. In doing so, they could live lives of purpose, becoming everything they want to be, not feel they need to be.

Now I understood the full meaning of my name and my entire life journey so far.

"If you can fly, then soar," I sang to myself, from Barbra Streisand's "A Piece of Sky." But instead of the song's last line, I sang: "Olopiro! The wind that lifts up a bird."

Acknowledgments

My Immediate Family

I think it's always best to start at the beginning of the journey. With this in mind, I would like to start by thanking my immediate family who shaped me as a person and put me on the path towards a good life. They taught me the value of love, community and the true meaning of family. As such, I am grateful for the following people:

Mom, Dad and Annie, you are, and *will* always be, the reason I am able to do what I do. You never gave up and neither will I. My grandparents, Jim and Rosemary Callas and Keith and Marjene West, Tammy and Bonnie Vavra, Diana and Desi Hoffman, Phillip, Jamie, Mitchell (who truly is awesome) and Emily (my god daughter) Krmpotich, Tony Corona and Auntie Paravicini. I'd like to thank the entire West family for their support and love over the last thirty years. Especially Steve

West for always having a joke and teaching me the importance of humor. As well as Reid and Jeanne West, Gaylen West and Verna West for their incredible support. I would also like to thank Greatgrandpa and Grandma Callas, Corona, West and Hansen for your sacrifices so we could have a better life. Last but not least, I want to thank Daisy (yes, I'm thanking my dog—if you met her you would, too) for teaching me love and patience.

U.S. Family

The following is a group of people whose hearts and souls have intertwined with mine along this journey. It is destiny that we found each other and our souls will continue to find each other long after we are gone.

John McMahan and Marci Cunningham, Reed Cowan (your mentorship and friendship means everything to me and I give thanks every day that you walked into that Old Navy ten years ago), Greg Abplanalp, Wesley Cowan and my godsons Asher and Kai Abplanalp-Cowan. I'd also like to thank Dan Nichols, Jenny Dagnino, Emily Dagnino, James Ruiz, Paul Gonzales, Sarah Combs, Tia Hill, Theresa Sarna, Tim Schrimer, Corrine Hopkins, the Old Navy crew in Sugarhouse and the Dolce crew.

Canadian Family

Never would I have dreamt that my family would have expanded from the U.S. to North America. In no particular order, I would like to thank my Canadian Family whose hearts and souls have also intertwined with mine.

To my sisters Leah "Midge" Ruinsky, Angelique de Montbrun, Sally Hakim, Sarah Young (we are both Canadians at heart), Simona Ramkisson, Erin Blanding, Giustina D'Elia, Emily Payne, Janice Sousa, Brooke Thompson, Robin Wiszowaty and Jodie Collins.

To my brothers David Johnson (I would be lost without you), Alex "Duckboy" Meers, Dean Delia (you will always be Canadian to me, even with an Australian accent), Matt Tod, Dan Mossip-Balkwill and Michel Chikwanine.

A special thank you to Ella and Arlo de Montburn Johnson for keeping me grounded and reminding me of the importance of taking the time to enjoy the small things.

Free The Children and Me to We Family

I would like to thank the entire staff at Me to We and Free The Children not only in Toronto, but in our regional and country offices, for the incredible work you do during the day, on the weekends and into the wee hours of the morning. A special thank you to Dwight Ireland and the speaking staff, the entire Me to We engagement team, Ryan Bolton, Sapna Goel, Matthew Ng, Hannah Feldberg, Maran Stern, the We Day team, Angie Gurley and the public relations team.

Mentors and Heroes

No journey would be complete without the guidance of mentors and heroes to challenge us and raise us up to more than we thought we could be.

I would like to thank The Shriners Hospital for Children, Cheryl Ruffini, Dave Hanks, Beth Whitman, Gigi Jasper, Vicki Vincent, Alan Keller, Michael and Nina Vought, Renee Hodgkinson, Marc Kielburger, Craig Kielburger, Roxanne Joyal, Jonathan and Shelley White, Chris and Tania Carnegie, Debbie Petrie Bullock, Jason Mraz, Ethan Zohn, Betty Williams and Rosie O'Donnell.

Most importantly, a heartfelt thank you to the incredible students around the world who work so hard to provide a better life for themselves and others. You are, and will always be, my true heroes.

I struggled with this section as there are so many people who have been instrumental in my journey thus far. Although I hope I didn't forget anyone, I probably did, so please consider this my thank you to those I may have left out. It wasn't intentional.

One last special thank you to Susan McClelland for helping me make my story come alive on the page. Thank you.

ABOUT SPENCER WEST

Spencer is an acclaimed motivational speaker with Me to We. Spencer's candid speeches about overcoming the struggles of losing his legs at age five have resonated with millions of people the world over. Spencer has shared the stage with Dr. Jane Goodall, former U.S. Vice President Al Gore, Mia Farrow, Reverend Jesse L. Jackson Sr., Nobel Peace Prize laureates Betty Williams and Elie Wiesel, and his musical idol Jason Mraz. This is Spencer's first book. He lives in Toronto.

ABOUT SUSAN McCLELLAND

Susan is the co-author of *The Bite of the Mango*, which has won numerous awards, including the 2011 Red Maple Award, the IBBY Outstanding Books for Young People with Disabilities, the 2009 Norma Fleck award and a gold award from the National Parenting Publications Awards. Her work has appeared in *Reader's Digest*, *Maclean's* magazine, *Times London*, *Glamour*, *Marie Claire*, *The Globe and Mail* and *The Walrus* magazine. In 2005 and 2008, she won the Amnesty International Media Award for excellence in human rights reporting. She splits her time between Toronto and Scotland, where much of her family now live.

About Free The Children

FREE THE CHILDREN
children helping children through education

Free The Children is the world's largest network of children helping children through education, with more than one million youth involved in our innovative education and development programs in 45 countries. Founded in 1995 by international child rights activist Craig Kielburger, we are a charity and educational partner that believes in a world where all young people are free to achieve their fullest potential as agents of change. Our domestic programs educate, engage and empower hundreds of thousands of youth in North America, the UK and around the world. Our international projects have brought over 650 schools and school rooms to youth and provided clean water, health care and sanitation to one million people around the world.

Visit **www.freethechildren.com** to find out more.

About Me to We

 me to we

Better choices for a better world

Me to We is an innovative social enterprise that provides people with better choices for a better world. Through socially conscious and environmentally friendly products and life-changing experiences, Me to We measures the bottom line, not by dollars earned, but by the number of lives we change and the positive social and environmental impact we make. In addition, half of Me to We's net profit is donated to Free The Children and the other half is reinvested to grow the enterprise.

Visit **www.metowe.com** to find out more.

Bring Spencer to your school

Bring a speaker to your child's school, your parent and educator association or your workplace conferences—and take away all you need to "be the change."

The team at Me to We has traveled the world to discover the most inspirational people with remarkable stories and life experiences. From community activists to former child soldiers to social entrepreneurs, our roster of energetic, experienced speakers are leading the Me to We movement: living and working in developing communities, helping businesses achieve social responsibility and inspiring auditoriums of youth and educators to action.

They leave audiences with a desire to take action and make a difference. They'll make you laugh, cry and gain new perspective on what really matters. Be warned: their passion is contagious!

Visit **www.metowe.com/speakers** to learn more.

Join Spencer on a Me to We Trip

If you want to really experience another culture and truly see the world, take a Me to We trip. Sure, you could lounge on yet another beach, surrounded by other stressed-out visitors seeing the usual tourist traps. But why not seek out a volunteer travel experience that radically changes your perspective, positively transforming the lives of others?

Our staff live and work in the communities you'll visit, coordinating schoolbuilding and supporting development in participation with local communities. On a Me to We trip, you'll learn leadership skills, experience new cultures and forge truly meaningful connections.

Over 3,000 adventurous people of all ages have chosen to volunteer abroad with us. You'll do incredible things, like build schools and assist on clean water projects. You'll meet exuberant children excited at new possibilities for learning, and be immersed in local communities.

You'll get your hands dirty digging wells and laying foundations. But you'll love it. You'll come home with a sunburn—and the biggest smile you've ever had on your face. And best of all, you'll have memories that last a lifetime.

Visit **www.metowe.com/trips** to learn more.

Books with a real message

The World Needs Your Kid

Craig and Marc Kielburger and Shelley Page

This unique guide to parenting is centered on a simple but profound philosophy that will encourage children to become global citizens. Drawing on life lessons from such remarkable individuals as Jane Goodall, Elie Wiesel and Archbishop Desmond Tutu, award-winning journalist Shelley Page and Marc and Craig Kielburger demonstrate how small actions make huge differences in the life of a child and can ultimately change the world.

Free the Children
Craig Kielburger

This is the story that launched a movement. *Free the Children* recounts 12-year-old Craig Kielburger's remarkable odyssey across South Asia, meeting some of the world's most disadvantaged children, exploring slums and sweatshops, fighting to rescue children from the chains of inhumane conditions.

My Maasai Life
Robin Wiszowaty

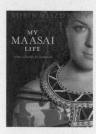

In her early 20s, Robin Wiszowaty left the ordinary world behind to join a traditional Maasai family. In the sweeping vistas and dusty footpaths of rural Kenya, she embraced a way of life unlike she'd ever known. With full-color photographs from her adventures, Robin's heart-wrenching story will inspire you to question your own definitions of home, happiness and family.

Take Action! A Guide to Active Citizenship
Craig and Marc Kielburger

Want to begin changing the world? *Take Action!* is a vivid, hands-on guide to active citizenship packed with the tools young people need to make a difference. Accomplished human rights activists Marc and Craig Kielburger share valuable tips and advice from their experiences as founders of Free The Children and the Me to We movement. Ideal for grades 8–10, *Take Action!* shows that young people don't need to wait to be the leaders of tomorrow—this journey begins now.

Take More Action: How to Change the World
Craig and Marc Kielburger with Deepa Shankaran

Ready to take the next step? *Take More Action* is our advanced guide to global citizenship, empowering young people to be world-changers—around the world or in their own backyard. Brilliantly illustrated and packed with powerful quotes, stories and resources, *Take More Action* includes invaluable material on character education, ethical leadership, effective activism and global citizenship. Ideal for Grades 10 and up, *Take More Action* paves the way for a lifetime of social action.

The Making of an Activist
Craig and Marc Kielburger with Lekha Singh

Warning: this book will change you. Full of vivid images and inspiring words, travelogues, poems and sparkling artwork, *The Making of an Activist* is more than just a scrapbook of Free The Children's remarkable evolution. It's a testament to living an engaged, active and compassionate life, painting an intimate portrait of powerful young activists. Explore the book. Catch the spark.

Global Voices, The Compilation: Vol. 1
Craig and Marc Kielburger

Global Voices aims to tell the untold stories of people and issues from around the world. With a foreword from Archbishop Tutu and discussion questions to help spark debate, this book will inspire young readers to deepen their understanding of issues and explore how they can change these headlines. Tied together from Craig and Marc's columns that have appeared in newspapers across Canada, *Global Voices* touches on the tough issues in an enlightening, enjoyable read.

Visit **www.metowe.com/books** to see our full list of bestselling books.

The Buy a Book, Give a Book promise ensures that for every Me to We book purchased, a notebook will be given to a child in a developing country.

Continue to follow Spencer on his journey...

twitter.com/Spencer2TheWest

facebook.com/Spencer2TheWest